American Ethics
and Public Policy

American Ethics
and Public Policy

ABRAHAM KAPLAN

GREENWOOD PRESS, PUBLISHERS
WESTPORT, CONNECTICUT

Library of Congress Cataloging in Publication Data

Kaplan, Abraham, 1918-
  American ethics and public policy.

  Reprint of the 1963 ed. published by Oxford
University Press, New York, in series: A Galaxy
book.
    1. National characteristics, American. 2. Po-
litical ethics. 3. United States--Moral conditions.
I. Title.
[E169.1.K315   1980]   172   80-12151
ISBN 0-313-22354-8 (lib. bdg.)

Originally published in *The American Style:
Essays in Value and Performance,* edited by Elting Morison
and published by Harper & Brothers, 1958

Five lines from "as freedom is a breakfastfood" by
E. E. Cummings, copyright 1940 by E. E. Cummings
Published in *Poems 1923-1954*
Reprinted by permission of Harcourt, Brace & World, Inc.

First published as a Galaxy Book, with corrections, 1963
by special arrangement with Harper & Row, Publishers,
Incorporated.

Reprinted with the permission of Harper and Row Publishers, Inc.

Reprinted in 1980 by Greenwood Press,
a division of Congressional Information Service, Inc.
51 Riverside Avenue, Westport, Connecticut 06880

Printed in the United States of America

10 9 8 7 6 5 4 3 2 1

To Mike
from whom I learned much ethics
and little policy

Contents

as freedom is a breakfastfood
or truth can live with right and wrong
or molehills are from mountains made
—long enough and just so long
will being pay the rent of seem

                    e. e. cummings

INTRODUCTION

Nowadays a writer must begin by showing his credentials, especially if he is writing on such things as morality and politics. The reader's psyche, its integrity threatened by an unceasing flow of news, news behind the news, analysis, interpretation, admonition, and appeal, has come to a system of security regulations for its own defense: no ideas admitted without appropriate clearance. It does not matter that the credentials will receive only a cursory glance or that, if scrutinized, they can be distinguished from the counterfeit only with the greatest difficulty. The important thing is to have the talisman. A writer who begins by announcing his viewpoint not only disarms suspicion, but may even find that he is taken at his own word. And if the announcement includes his presuppositions, frames of reference, and (holy name!) methodology, scarcely anything more need be said; success with the reader is assured. Americans love frankness, and a freely admitted fault is almost better than unvarying virtue. Academically, remission of sin needs only confession, not penance.

But there is an academic sin which cannot be forgiven, the sin against specialization. Every writer must be an expert, and every expert must write only on his own specialty—unless, to be sure, there has been ritual expiation by communion in an interdisciplinary project. Each expert thereby partakes mystically of the expertness of all the rest, and the failings of each become the virtues of all. But setting out alone, as I am, I approach the reader burdened with a presumption of guilt. Is this

3

an essay in the history of ideas? I am not a historian. Does it purport to delineate American culture or to categorize American politics? I am neither sociologist nor political scientist. If the essay deals with matters of fact at all, where are my surveys, polls, and interviews, my tables and graphs, clinical observations, and experimental results? And if it presents only relations of ideas, where are my postulates, definitions, demonstrations? If it does neither, must it not be committed to Humean flames as sophistry and illusion?

Alas, it does neither—and both; responsive, I hope, to fact, and contributing, as I hope again, to a clearer conceptualization of fact. Yet not limited to these, but setting out also what I prize and condemn— judgments of value where I have succeeded, and caprice or crotchet masquerading as judgment where I have failed. And more too: what is praised or censured is so presented as to invite like-mindedness; and perhaps even fragments of a metaphysics of man and nature strategically placed to hide the nakedness of personal valuation. How each sentence in what follows is to be classed in these categories—or perhaps in categories more felicitous though less commendable—I leave to others. If I must bear the responsibility for such bastard discourse, why then, I suppose I must. A man cannot moralize for others and expect to go scot free himself.

Here is a reason for demanding credentials of a writer on morals and politics. There can be today no moral ventriloquism, no speaking for a pretended consensus or with a mock authority that deceives no one. The reader wants to know, and rightly, whom he can hold responsible; the critic wants the address of next of kin. The fact is that there are specialists in morality, too; the American division of labor is detailed and thorough. There are priests, social workers, and psychiatrists. There are administrators of moral codes for industries and professions. There are even associations organized to promote and defend the moral decencies. There are, indeed, so many experts of this breed that their very number makes identification all the more imperative. Morality is relative to the person of the moralizer. Relativity is the great Boyg around which contemporary ethics cannot go, subjectivity the Mountain King.

To theorize about values—so runs the tale—is scarcely more than to rationalize the moralities (or lack of them) that we have bound to our Gyntish selves, and the sovereignties to which we have vowed allegiance by submitting to a nick of the eyeball. If thereafter, we squint, we can all the more easily share with Rousseau the joy of discovering in our researches on government new reasons for loving that of our own country, with Kant the awe at the grandeur of the moral law which we ourselves have given to ourselves, and with Hegel the confidence that our state is the highest embodiment of universal reason that history has as yet unfolded.

But theorizing is not to be trusted; in the perversity of too much cleverness, what if we were to find reasons for skepticism? Cotton Mather records in his diary that "the employing of so much time upon Ethics in our colleges" is not only "very unwise," but indeed, "a vile 'Piece of Paganism,'"[1] and Charles Peirce, closer by half to our day than to Mather's, observes that "nothing makes a man so much of a scoundrel as a prolonged study of ethics." To be sure, writers on America have not distinguished themselves for dwelling on whatever things are lovely and of good report—with the occasional exceptions of some "intellectuals" who have wished to dissociate themselves from that dissociated class. We must look on the good as well as on the bad, neither in self-justification nor as sitting in judgment on others, but because the good is the only resource by which the bad can be transformed.

But "good" and "bad"—is this not still to say, my good and bad? There is no help for it, I must identify myself: by training a positivist, by inclination a pragmatist, in temperament a mystic, in practice a Democrat; my faith Jewish, educated by the Catholics, an habitual protestant; born in Europe, raised in the Midwest, hardened in the East, and softened once more in California; psychoanalyzed, naturalized, denatured—in short, an American academician.

Most American, perhaps, in the respects in which I am most aberrant; for America is so multiple, so varied and vast, that only the deviant is truly representative. On the morals of politics there are not two parties but hundreds, differing in region and religion, caste and class, ethnic origin and personal destination. If we were to blur these differences by appealing to a "national character," that would but be, as Max Weber warned, "a mere confession of ignorance."[2] Yet the mind must have its universals, subsuming the many under an abstract unity. "Of course the one American I speak of," Santayana confesses, "is mythical; but to speak in parables is inevitable in such a subject, and it is perhaps as well to do so frankly." [3] In such a subject, perhaps the speaker himself is inevitably something of a parable.

I ask, then, of this mythical American, what is his way of good and evil? what he does, his morals; what he says or thinks he does, his moral code; the theories and principles with which he justifies or rationalizes both, his ethics; and, of course, what he *should* do and why he should do it, my code and ethics but also, in intention at least, my judgment of a truth that lies outside me.

But in such questions to link morals with politics might be thought to be yoking together an ox and an ass—morality is one thing, political action another. Not so. Morality covers the area of prizing of the human personality, in the self and in others, and its province is as wide as all action bearing on man's worth—which is to say, as wide as all man does. Political morality is not a matter only of bribery and corruption, fraud and venality, or their absence. It is not a private possession making from time to time a public appearance when the private citizen holds public office. It is intrinsic to all policy whose decisions significantly affect the value placed on things human. Public morality is the morality of public policy.

In what follows I try to sketch an experimental basis for this morality. While insisting on the historical importance for American democracy of religious doctrines and the metaphysics of "natural rights," I reject the widespread assumptions that without such transcendent faiths the belief in democracy is untenable, and that the future of democracy therefore rests on a "spiritual" revival. On the contrary, I am persuaded that the divorce of the spirit from the matter of daily experience itself endangers moral values. It is in this dualism of transcendent ideals and earthly expediences that I localize the degradation of our political life. What is needed is not more idealism, but more realistic ideals; not exhortations to an abstract virtue, but support of concrete measures for the betterment of specific situations.

In this perspective I also criticize moral absolutism, the pretense that the right and the good are unequivocal and certain, and that they are realizable in every case by unswerving adherence to high principle. Yet the rejection of absolutism still allows, as I hope, a place for principled action, and even for moral heroism. Only, I have urged that it is not principles themselves on which morality requires a firm stand, but rather the concrete values to which moral principles are instrumental. Our democracy has assumed too defensive a posture. Because we are determined not to take the offensive in a military sense, we tend to withdraw from the ideological offensive as well.[4] We underplay the positive content of democratic values; national defense becomes the substance of national ideals. The Oxford don who was asked during the First World War what he was contributing to the war effort replied, "Sir, I represent the civilization you are fighting to preserve." Events may have proved him mistaken; but only in his identification of the ends sought, not in his insistence that for a democracy military superiority cannot be an end in itself. I want to redirect attention from the communist threat to the democratic values that are threatened.

The moral failings with which I charge our political life are, I suppose, somewhat less in actuality than I may make them out to be, in defense of my own emotional investments. I must rely on the reader to introduce whatever corrections seem to him to yield a more balanced assessment. Undoubtedly the cultural lag from which philosophy inevitably suffers will have made my account somewhat anachronistic—less true of America today than it might have been a few years ago. Certainly a recent series of decisions in the federal courts, as well as various acts of Congress and Executive orders, mark a significant revitalization of our political morality. Were I to enlarge the frame in which I am here picturing American life so as to include other patterns than the narrowly political, my somber coloring would surely need to be brightened; the politics of conformism, for example, by no means implies a corresponding conformity in all the details of personal life, at any rate in the perspectives of a Californian!

Yet the passion for accuracy in every detail might properly be forced to yield to other passions. However comforting it might be, I cannot find it in myself to believe in a pre-established harmony between the true and the good. Discords between what values project as facts and what facts hold up as values recur over and over again, and must be resolved over and over again. Such resolutions are the very stuff of the moral life, and how to achieve them provides the terms in which every moral problem is posed. I make no claim that my account of American public policy is wholly true or that my ideal for American ethics is wholly good. But I am convinced that even a fragmentary truth may find its uses for a greater good.

METAPHYSICAL FOUNDATIONS OF AMERICAN VALUES

An interconnection of morals and politics has characterized ethical theory from the outset: whether because, as in Plato, the state is the individual writ large; or because, as with Aquinas, it has a moral aim; whether it is the source of morality, as for Hobbes; guided by a moral principle, as in the utilitarians' conception; or serves as the instrumentality for morals, as the pragmatists have it. In one way or another, theorists have persistently linked public and private morality.

Even more, they have urged that some ethical theory or other lies at the basis of political practice. They have looked into politics and, being philosophers, have found therein—a philosophy. On the political arena they have traced the outlines of their own shadows. So today there is much pretentious talk to the effect that the issues we face are at bottom metaphysical issues, that our political uncertainties reflect epistemological confusion, that world peace is attainable only through a world philosophy. In this respect, at any rate, American hard-headedness and practicality is largely a myth. There is widespread veneration for abstract "principles," philosophical foundations, some bedrock on which social policy can be firmly grounded. In a culture where values are not experienced as "given," there is a felt need for philosophical justifications. Armed with a philosophy, a man can feel doubly secure. The incantation has its own efficacy; should it fail, the pundits will provide him with more powerful wizardry. It is comforting to know that such assistance is available for the asking; being a sage is also a specialty at the service of the public.

But the claims that each philosophy makes for itself are significantly weakened by the counterclaims made by conflicting philosophies. For Walter Lippmann, liberal democracy is "unworkable" save by adherence to the philosophy of natural law in which it was conceived and founded. But Croce, being an idealist, finds that it is idealism "which is one with the liberal concept of life," and to be contrasted with "naturalism, positivism, and scientific principles, all associated with the authoritarian concepts or leading to them." On the other hand, Dewey is convinced of "the undoubted historic fact that the whole modern liberal social and political movement has allied itself with philosophic empiricism." Maritain is certain that only Catholic Christianity can justify a belief in the democratic charter; and a recent European analyst of the psychology of democracy and dictatorship finds in some type of neo-Kantianism "one of the most adequate expressions, at the philosophical level, of the cultural climate of democracy." [5] Can it be that only some happy few stand firm in their democratic convictions, while the rest have built on sand?

That there is some connection between underlying philosophies and political practice need not be doubted—philosophies do matter. The question now is whether the connection is a logical one. Can we speak here of "basic premises"? Is the truth of the philosophy a necessary or even sufficient condition for the truth or rightness of the politics which appeals to it? No. The so-called "premises" serve instead as idols of the theater or, in the current idiom, as defense mechanisms, deflecting responsibility from the citizen to a system, rationalizing personal choice as the logical outcome of shared principles. Concrete policy can be deduced from abstract philosophy only if the latter is rich in normative ambiguity, so that it can be taken in one reading as a truth of man and nature, and in another as formulating a norm of good and evil. With such equivocation in the premises, questions of policy can be gracefully begged.

Charles Stevenson has described the technique of "persuasive definition" so often applied to this end.[6] If Hegelian principles define "freedom" as obedience to the state, lovers of freedom can be given reasons for such obedience; and what is distressing, such reasons may be most effective. What leads to belief, and thereby action, is a very different thing from what entails belief. The range of policies to which a principle may lead and which it is believed to justify is limited in practice only by the skills of the ideologue and by the predispositions of his audience. Dostoevski's Grand Inquisitor was able to "prove" that he was acting entirely on the principles of his Prisoner; if we remain unconvinced, it is not because we reject the premises or because we detect a non sequitur, but because we are no longer mediaevals.

If abstract principles are not logically sufficient, for concrete policy, neither are they politically necessary. The United Nations Universal Declaration of Human Rights was subscribed to by representatives of

Vedanta and positivism, Buddhism and pragmatism, Christianity and neo-Confucianism. Was only one, at most, consistent? In his introduction to the UNESCO volume on *Human Rights*, Maritain writes: "If both believed in the democratic charter, a Christian and a rationalist would still give mutually incompatible justifications for their belief. . . . And God forbid that I should say that it does not matter to know which of the two is right! It matters essentially. The fact remains that, on the practical expression of this charter they are in agreement and can formulate together common principles of action." [7] It is this fact which is of the first importance: that there can be agreement on policy without agreement on what is called "the underlying philosophy." But if such agreement extends throughout the entire range of policy affected by the philosophies, if the two are at one in all their "practical expressions," I find it hard to see why the difference makes any difference at all, to say nothing of an "essential" one.

As a matter of political and psychological fact, it is absurd to argue that values cannot be preserved if their "metaphysical basis" is repudiated. And as a matter of logic, the argument is trivial, for the "basis" can be nothing other than a statement of the values themselves transposed into a metaphysical key. Confusion here, as Sidney Hook has often pointed out, incurs the penalty of putting ideological obstacles in the way of agreement on the plane of action. And in some quarters it may provide a rationale for thought control on behalf of that ultimate absurdity: an "official" philosophy of democracy.

Has philosophy, then, come to this, that those who profess it do so only to proclaim its futility? Not at all! Futile only as a body of ultimate truths from which values are to be deduced; indispensable as a loosely knit texture of perspectives within which action finds meaning, both as significance and as worth. What matters is the philosophy lived by, commitment as well as conceptualization. And that philosophy, what makes for each man his experience intelligible and his life worth while, is not an abstract doctrine but a part of all that he has met. It is a product of the whole of culture and character—all the institutions which shape his actions, all the habits which canalize them, all the impulses which give them substance: in science, religion, art, industry, and in politics as well. The search for a philosophy of politics is a search, not just for ultimate premises, but for conclusions, too. And perhaps most of all, it is a search for those inferential links by which each man can fasten together all he knows and loves and bind it to the fabric of his life among other men. Such a search no man can carry out for another, and what is found answers only to his own seeking. In America, three main paths have been followed: through a social religion, through moral intuition, and through empirical science. I shall consider them in turn.

It is not to be forgotten that the liberty in which this nation was conceived was in important measure a religious liberty. To be sure, the Thanksgiving ritual is not altogether a paradigm of Colonial history; but the airy fancies of the folk myth are no more fanciful than the stony mythology of economic determinism. Economic, political, social forces —what you will; but the religious impulse, too, played its part, and it was more than an off-stage voice. The liberty sought, it is true, was often for a single sect, and that one's own; the victim of Old World intolerance sometimes, alas, avenged himself in the New. Yet toleration spread, and though sectarian faith, as the orthodox had feared, was thereby weakened, in the aggregate it waxed great. The number of denominations in America today is to be counted, not in the dozens, but in the hundreds.

Church membership, however, may owe more to the fact that we are a nation of joiners than to our being a fellowship of the devout. Yet on the American political scene religion is prominent far beyond any measure of churched and unchurched citizens. Particularly is this true of political symbolism, Merriam's "miranda" of politics.[8] Within the last decade our oath of allegiance proclaimed us to be one nation "under God"; our coinage has long reposed its trust in the treasures laid up in Heaven as well as in the Federal Reserve; our Congress enters upon its deliberations only after assurance that its proceedings will be viewed with interest from heights even above the press galleries. And a recent distinguished statesman is perhaps less likely to be remembered for his legislative wisdom than because, known to have had presidential aspirations, he died speaking the words: "I had rather be a servant in the house of the Lord than sit in the seats of the mighty."

To suppose that in politics all this is no more than rhetoric is to forget that in government by discussion politics *is* a manner of speaking. If a candidate for office cannot risk publicly dissociating himself from religion, something of political importance is involved. Even if candidate and electorate alike are pretending to a concern neither feels, a genuine force is at work to maintain the pretence. How great this force is has been attested to innumerably: Bryce and Myrdal, separated by more than half a century, are able to agree in the flat assessment that religion is probably more influential in America than in any other country.[9]

And its influence is not a matter of symbols only, however important these may be, but a matter of practices as well. American religion is not mystic and monastic, but follows the social gospel. It may recoil from humanism in its faith, but its works are frankly humanitarian. Unlike what has happened in many theocentric or transcendental religions of Europe and Asia, here moral values have become at least as significant for the church as distinctively spiritual ones. Perhaps this marks the substitution of a moral faith for a religious one. At any rate, the consequence is that for many Americans religion is indeed something to live by. In the last century, three of the major churches split on the issue of slavery; today, integration marks another area of religious relevance.[10] Yet it is not merely an easy cynicism which notes the disparity between creed and performance.

Not just action, but the perspectives in which action acquires significance, what I called the working philosophies, bear in America the unmistakable marks of religious patterns. Bryce goes so far as to say that "the prevalence of evangelical Protestantism has been quite as important a factor in the intellectual life of the nation as its form of government." [11] Certainly the dominant American philosophies, idealism and pragmatism, are both indeed evangels, bearers of glad tidings, holding out the promise of salvation by resolute loyalty to ideal purposes. The story is that when Emerson Hall was built at Harvard to house the philosophy department, James proposed for it the inscription, "Man is the measure of all things"; but he was overruled by his colleague, Royce, who countered with, "What is man that Thou art mindful of him?" Both agreed, however, in seeing man as the locus of vast potentialities, and the world as limitless in its possibilities for good. These are the perspectives of American religion, and of American politics as well.

In such perspectives, political values are put on a spiritual basis, political morality is objectified as a product of divine will. Liberty is God-given, equality is the leveling of man in the eyes of God, fraternity is God's injunction to love our neighbor. "Can the liberties of a nation be thought to be secure when we have removed their only firm basis, a conviction in the minds of the people that their liberties are the gift of God?" This question was asked, not by a minister of the church, but by Thomas Jefferson. Statesmen join with the ministry in deriving social legislation from the words of Job: "If I did despise the cause of my man-servant, or of my maid-servant, when they contended with me— what then shall I do when God rises up? . . . Did not He that made me make him? And did not one God fashion us both?" [12] The brotherhood of man is annually deduced in every pulpit from the common fatherhood of God.

Such deductions signify more than homiletic embellishment. The classic postulates of democratic theory affirm the existence of an objective difference between good and evil, and the capacity of every citizen to distinguish them and to choose freely between them. The religious philosophies account for the difference by reference to a divine order, and for the capacity to distinguish and choose by reference to conscience and free will. The dependence of democracy on religion in America is not, as is sometimes argued, that democracy lives only by the faith in it of its citizens, and faith is all of a piece. Such talk, equivocating on "faith," establishes connections of fact only by obscuring distinctions of meaning. Only verbal trickery can identify the weakening of a faith in God with a loss of that faith in man that democracy calls for. The point is that religion in America, or the dominant Protestantism at any rate, insists that man is in no need of humanly authoritative guidance and help to find the truth and thereby to attain the good. It is this insistence that constitutes the democratic faith: that men are not so depraved, so ignorant, or so helpless as not to be trusted with the making of their own lives. The reliance that each individual may put in his own conscience in matters of religion is easily generalized to a political individualism. The inviolability of each man's firmness in the right as God gives him to see the right finds its counterpart in the dignity of the free citizen as the source and not just the subject of state authority.

Thus a religious man, committed to democratic values, can interpret them in religious terms, and in America has usually done so. But religious beliefs alone cannot compel him to such values. That men are equal in the eyes of God does not of itself entail that they must be so in the eyes of the state: earthly inequalities may be among those things which the faithful must render unto Caesar. The church which prizes the dignity of each man's soul may call upon the secular arm to destroy his body for the sake of his soul. In human history deprivation of life and liberty, to say nothing of interference with the pursuit of happiness, has been justified rather more often by appeal to divine law than by reference solely to a civil order.[13] The relation between political morality and religious faith is not that either can be deduced from the other, but that, in man's urge toward coherent and comprehensive perspectives of action, both political aspirations and religious ideals are shaped and strengthened by the realms of value disclosed in the other.

I do not see, therefore, that democratic conclusions can be denied, as a matter either of logic or of psychology, to those who reject the religious premises from which some persons mistakenly suppose such conclusions to be derived. It is said that Bertrand Russell, in a public lecture at Cooper Union, was once asked, "Lord Russell, how do you account for the fact that, though all men were created equal, there is so much injustice in the world?" To which he promptly replied, "Well, you see, I don't believe that men were created at all!" The religious premise carries with it only a religious conclusion, not a political one; and a morality is entailed by it only when the morality has been presupposed.

But such a presupposition can as easily be secular as sacred. If we must first believe men to be created equal in order to justify the ideal of political equality, can we not just as well believe to start with that men are equal in their own nature, and thus base our political ethics on a natural rather than a supernatural order? In American thought this alternative has been an even more influential conception of the ground of value, for both man and the state, than the purely religious one. Explicitly formulated, it constitutes the theory of natural rights and natural law.

Some such theory has played a part in many of the world's great religious philosophies. By it, religion is naturalized, and the supernatural projected onto the face of nature as a principle of cosmic order. The Law of Heaven reaches down into life on earth as the injunction to maintain this order. The *tao* of Chinese philosophy, *dharma* in Indian thought, the *torah* of the Hebrews, and *ananke* of the Greeks are from this point of view variations on a single theme. In all, moral obligation and natural necessity are fused into a conception of a system of nature which accommodates both facts and values. Fundamentally, the principle of value lies in the orderliness of the facts: when all is in place, the outcome is a cosmic equilibrium reflected in man's mind as the idea of justice. Wrongdoing is an upsetting of the balance, a departure from the path on which alone righteousness lies.

Such a system of nature may find its political counterpart in a fixed social order, a hierarchy of positions each of which carries a determinate set of rights and duties. Crime and sin coincide as *hubris*, not knowing one's place. Natural law here becomes the ideology of conservatism and absolutism, as in Aquinas and Hobbes. The violation of the natural order, so conceived, was the basis of Greek tragedy. But as the fixities of the social order are dissolved, such violations may become the matter of comedy. The tragic victim of fate in Sophocles gives way in Shaw to the comic hero who disregards social roles.

For the system of nature may be thought to be reflected, not in society as such, but in the microcosm of the individual mind. In this perspective, shared rationality binds men together in universal brotherhood, while endowing each individual with inviolable rights grounded in his own rational nature. Such a philosophy lends itself to a liberal society where obligations are freely contracted by each individual, not deduced from a preassigned status. This is the conception of natural law running through the Stoics, Spinoza, Locke, and thence to the founders of the American republic.

The objective difference between good and evil called for by the religionist is here provided in a more economical metaphysics by the natural order. Governments exist to secure the rights which by nature belong to the governed; political morality consists in the scrupulous acknowledgment of these rights. The Declaration of Independence demands for the American people only "the separate and equal station to which the Laws of Nature and of Nature's God entitle them." In the same vein, though not so explicitly, the preamble of the Universal Declaration of Human Rights adopted by the General Assembly of the United Nations affirms that "recognition of the inherent [sic] dignity and of the equal and inalienable [sic] rights of all members of the human family is the foundation of freedom, justice and peace in the world." And Article One lays it down that "all human beings are born [sic] free and equal in dignity and rights." Natural law, though not a premise for the deduction of political rights, is in America and throughout the contemporary world an acknowledged platform of political aspiration to such rights.[14]

The theory of natural rights, in its modern setting, can be understood as an extension of the religious right of emancipation from institutional authority. "Every man his own priest" leads easily to the principle of "every man a king." The primacy of the individual conscience, read out into nature as an objectified system of norms, accounts for the distinctive traits of the law of nature. Natural law is self-evident as a deliverance of moral intuition, irrevocable as sharing in the binding force of a self-imposed moral obligation, universal as the moral standard which is applied to the self only as holding for all men everywhere. Natural law is not the ground of political morality but its projective expression.

For the "nature" of the theory is not the nature disclosed to empirical inquiry, but what is identified as "natural" in the sense of conforming to a norm externally imposed. Is it "natural" for a mother to deprive her children, or a ruler his loyal subjects, of their lives and liberties? Such things have been done. Nature as the totality of observed and observable fact includes the violation of every "natural right" and "natural law" that political theorists have laid down. The "nature" of the theory is only what answers to the norms of the theorizer; it is these norms, not nature herself, from which the political rights are derived. "A great multitude of people are continually talking of the Law of Nature," Bentham observes, "and then they go on giving you their sentiments about what is right and wrong; and these sentiments, you are to understand, are so many chapters and sections of the Law of Nature." [15] We who condemn despotism and injustice must ourselves assume the responsibility for the code of political morality by which we judge them to be damnable.

The whole apparatus of natural law adds nothing to the moral content of our politics, but only changes its form of expression. Beginning with whatever code of political rights and duties our needs and knowledge, traditions and experience have produced, we covertly construct from it a system of natural law, present this as objective in origin and universal in application, then triumphantly derive from it the rights and duties with which we started. The futility of such logic was clearly seen by Hume: ". . . How fruitless it is to . . . seek in the laws of nature a stronger foundation for our political duties than interest and human conventions, while these laws (the laws of nature) themselves are built on the very same foundation." We walk this circle only because, if it be sufficiently great, we can return convinced that we stand at the still point of the turning world. Rights to be defended as our ideals and secured through our efforts can then be seen as antecedently guaranteed, absolute and fixed in the nature of things. Such a conviction may indeed produce a show of courage: with a stacked deck a man will stake everything. But when we are challenged by competing absolutes, the courage called for must have deeper roots, or it will vanish.

Of itself, then, natural law has no definite content; the morality it proclaims is the product of moral intuition, not of metaphysical deduction. Now the fact is that intuitions differ. However much we may insist that what is intuited is a law outside the self, as fixed in its own character as are the principles of science and mathematics discerned by sense and reason, the question still remains which of several conflicting moralities has properly intuited its object. And this question intuition alone cannot answer, but can only beg. If conscience speaks to each man the word of the one God, what a pity she speaks in so many different tongues! Indeed, when it comes to conscience, a man may fail to understand even his native accents. The oracle must perforce speak in riddles when the God within is Himself of two minds.

Moreover, the law of nature claims to rest on what is innate in man, not on what is imposed or withheld by merely human institutions. But habit becomes second nature, and natural law must inevitably change as men become habituated to changed institutions. Moral sensibility is notoriously capable of being blunted: vice, we have been warned, may be first endured, then pitied, then embraced. An all-powerful state need not fear the moral intuitions of its citizenry; it can shape these intuitions to its own ends, as a succession of modern novelists have pictured with fearful realism. It is easy to see how natural law may be made matter for indoctrination; not so easy to conceive of a process of education of the faculty on which its recognition depends, without presupposing the infallibility of the educator.

In sum, we need not wonder that in American history natural rights and natural law have been argued on behalf of the most diverse policies: by Federalists and anti-Federalists, slaveholders and abolitionists, reformers and reactionaries. For the "nature" appealed to was not given in experience, but imposed on experience to accord with pre-determined values. "The views held regarding human nature," John Dewey has observed, "were those appropriate to the purposes and policies a given group wanted to carry through. . . . What passed as psychology was a branch of political doctrine." [16] And the same is true of what passed as the metaphysics of political morality.

EMPIRICAL FOUNDATIONS OF AMERICAN VALUES

The theory of natural law has content only in association with some specific political doctrine, a set of values determining, in a concrete situation, a concrete social policy. But if the theory does not give these values a metaphysical ground, it does put them in a special class. In calling rights "natural" it makes for them a claim quite out of the ordinary. Can we interpret this claim in empirical rather than metaphysical terms? Can natural rights be truly naturalized, made all of a piece with the stuff of concrete experience? I believe they can; and what is more, I believe that in American history the theory has largely been used in this empirical sense. Perhaps we should say that we have here, not one conception of political ethics, but two, finding expression in the same words. It is an axiom of practical semantics that not words but uses determine meanings. Talk of "natural" rights does not of itself commit politics to a transcendent metaphysics, just as talk of "experience" does not make politics genuinely empirical.

What, then, might be meant, in terms of everyday experience, by calling a right "natural"? Surely, that it is in some sense a fundamental right, of prime importance, basic to other rights. This would not be true of a right resulting from some special agreement—I mean a real agreement, not the myth of a social contract. Such a right would be enjoyed only by the parties to the agreement and would be subject to the conditions set by the terms of the agreement. To call a right "natural" is to characterize it as presupposed by agreements, like the right to expect agreements to be kept. It is to characterize it as not dependent on any voluntary act of the claimant to the right or indeed of any person whatever. There is a legend that at the moment of birth there is revealed to each soul its fate on earth, and the soul is offered a final choice of remaining in its heavenly home. In sober fact there is no such choice; as the wag has it, it is much better never to have been born at all, but not one man in ten thousand has such luck. A right is "natural," not as literally innate, a concomitant of birth, but as not acquired by subsequent choice. Man, if he is free at all, must be born free, for he could not choose freedom unless first he were free to choose.

But could not freedom be conferred on him from without? This, too, is just what is denied in placing freedom among the natural rights. A right is "natural" rather than "conventional" in the sense of belonging to a man in his own capacity and not as related to other men. But this need not mean that natural law is outside of and antecedent to society, as Hobbes argued; outside some human relatedness there are no men at all. It may mean, rather, in the spirit of Locke, that such law is basic to social living, that it is the fundamental law, that it provides, in a word, what Americans call the Constitution for the society. The metaphysical interpretation stands the logic of experience on its head. Natural rights are not specified in a constitution because they are natural; they are natural because a constitution specifies them.

Of course, it is not a written constitution that is in question here. Americans put altogether too much weight on the written word. What matters is the complex of predispositions and practices that are expressed in and sustained by constitutional formulae. And these patterns of valuation and action come to this: that politics is subordinate to morals. Political enactments are subject to moral appraisal, not the other way about. The appeal to natural law is a reminder that politics is not autonomous: human law must justify itself before the bar of natural justice. What is important is not that this standard is "natural" in some metaphysical sense, but that it is not political in the plain everyday sense. One of the cartoons of this century shows a helpless citizen being beaten by a thug in a storm trooper's uniform; the caption reads: "Yuh want da police? I'm da police!" The theory of natural law, in its experiential meaning, amounts to the insistence, not that there *is*, in a world of pure idea, but that there *ought* to be, on this bloody earth, another court of appeal. The metaphysics of "nature" ontologizes ideals, and takes "ought" for "is" to escape a painful "should."

The rights of nature are inalienable because in calling them "natural" we express our determination not to allow their alienation. The belief in natural law is a tissue of commitment to other men, but even more to our moral selves. The "nature" appealed to is not the object of a cognition from which a valuation is deduced, but is itself made up of what is valued. The "laws of nature" have always been closely linked with "nature's God," and in the religious idiom, to know God is not other than to love Him, and those who deny Him live in a hell of their own making, for they deny themselves.

As I read Spinoza and the Stoics, this is the great insight in their appeal to nature. Freedom is of man's essence, for only one who is already sunk in human bondage can agree not to be his own master. You may put my body in prison, but not me, says Epictetus; he did not conceive of the power of the modern totalitarian state to imprison men's minds as well. Yet somehow he was right: God made men upright even though they have sought out many inventions. It is this truth of man's own makeup that the theory of natural rights obliquely expresses. One who is truly free owes his freedom to no man.

But he does owe to others something of the self which, in its maturity, achieves such freedom. Here, I think, is the root error of romantic individualism. Rousseau proclaims, in the opening words of his *Social Contract*, that "man is born free yet he is everywhere in chains." But man is individuated only in society. What is born is a cluster of potentialities, and societies allow now some, now others, to reach actuality. If we are to speak of birth literally, Aristotle is more consistent in holding some men born to be masters and others slaves. We say in America that freedom is an "inalienable" right in the insistence that it is this potentiality in all men which is to become actual. But the insistence is ours, not nature's, and it acquires meaning in experience only as we have the courage and wisdom to imitate "nature" in our social arts. The Declaration which begins with an appeal to the law of nature ends with a pledge of lives, fortunes, and sacred honor.

Natural rights, then, are an achievement, not a heritage. It is the blunting of this point in the attempt to justify these values by referring them to a basis in "nature" which is a danger to democratic values. But once it is recognized that endless vigilance and courage are needed to secure these rights, the question of how they are to be justified is of no great moment. It gives way, instead, to the question of how they are to be known: their truth will appear in their verification. And the fact is that, whatever their source, they are known only in experience. Correspondingly, it is by reference to their outcome, not to their origins, that we judge them.

The founders of the American republic, sons of the Enlightenment, spoke the language of their century, and that was the language of "nature." But the doctrine they spoke in that language was in significant degree an empirical one. "Experience is the oracle of truth; and where its responses are unequivocal, they ought to be conclusive and sacred." These are the words, not of a doctrinaire empiricist, but of Hamilton and Madison, in No. XX of the *Federalist Papers*. Jefferson over and over again speaks of this government as "an experiment." And the Declaration of Independence, having laid against British rule the charge of an absolute tyranny, concludes its opening paragraphs with the sentence, "To prove this, let Facts be submitted to a candid world"— facts, not dialectical reasonings or deliverances of intuition. And, indeed, it continues with twenty-seven paragraphs detailing specific wrongs and injuries which justify the declared separation. The natural right of the people is a right to institute a government founded "on such principles . . . as to them shall seem most likely to effect their Safety and Happiness." Such a likelihood can ultimately be grounded only in experience.

But does this say anything more than that experience dictates the choice of means for given ends? Experience may show that separation is necessary to the "safety and happiness" of the American colonies; can it show that the colonists have a right to these things? It will not do to argue, as the utilitarians did, that "right" and "good" mean nothing more than this. To argue in this way is to be guilty of what G. E. Moore called the "naturalistic fallacy." Unless words like "happiness" are so construed as to be completely empty (and they often are!), we can always ask, but is the pursuit of that *particular* happiness morally right? For democracy makes a particular claim: it defines the aim of the state, not as the welfare of a race, nation, or class, but as the happiness of its individual citizens. And *this* end cannot in turn be justified by a definition.

An empirical theory of value must hold that ends as well as means are empirically judged. This is the position expounded in American life most influentially by John Dewey.[17] Every valuation is grounded in an evaluation; we are justified in prizing only what emerges as worthy from an empirical appraisal. The injunctions of morality cannot be divided, as Kant assumed, into hypothetical imperatives and categorical imperatives. At bottom they are all hypothetical, and only experience can warrant the presumed connection between hypothetical antecedent and enjoined consequent.

On this view, moral imperatives can be intelligently arrived at and maintained only after full exposure—directly, or mediated by transmitted knowledge—to facts concerning the conditions and consequences of the values involved. To be sure, such imperatives, serving as norms of action, are not propositional in form, and so cannot be certified as true, whether on an experiential basis or on any other. But American philosophy today avails itself of a technique known as the *method of coordination*. To each imperative there is coordinated a set of declarative propositions, and it is the truth of these propositions that provides the basis for the imperative. It cannot be denied that on the contemporary philosophic scene so-called "cognitivists" and "emotivists" differ from one another on the question whether the coordination exhausts the content of the norm. Does the imperative also have a noncognitive "emotive meaning," or does its cognitive content leave a residue only of a normative use? But more and more it is coming to be felt that the significance of this difference has been exaggerated by academic debate, a fruitless polemic in the name of labels and schools. There is widespread agreement that, whether in the last analysis or only penultimately, facts are of overriding relevance to values.

What truth attaches to a moral norm? By what coordination can it be given cognitive meaning? There is first its *reflexive* sense, that those who enjoin the imperative are themselves committed to the values it holds out. The values of a propagandist are false because they are insincere, insincere not as a matter of individual psychology but of political commitment. A master morality is false because it serves only to create a population of docile slaves: thou shalt, but not *I* will. And whether a morality is reflexively true is a question of fact, though the fact be hard to come by when minds are corrupted and the incorruptible are silenced.

There is second the *derived* cognitive meaning of implicit hypotheticals, that adequacy of means to ends which justifies the normative use of the categorical. We make one choice rather than another because of the consequences experience has led us to expect—consequences on character and personality, to be sure, as well as on the material world, but consequences rooted in experience nevertheless. The necessity of the moral law is at bottom the ineluctability of fact. We must, because, the world being what it is, we have no choice. Nature, to be commanded, must be obeyed, and obedience to the moral law is the condition of power over such values as life affords.

And there is third the extended cognitive meaning of a moral imperative which consists in the fittingness to its object of the attitude and emotion expressed by it. To value something is to take up a certain attitude toward it, but attitudes are not compartmentalized from beliefs. Our emotions are not withdrawn into themselves, but reach out into the world and are rational only as the world goes out to meet them in turn. Joy and sorrow, love and fear, all the substance of our moral life, may be groundless in particular circumstances, as ignorance, error, prejudice, and confusion seal us off from the world as it truly is. Whether they are well grounded in given circumstances is again a question of fact.

In short, an empirical theory of value judges by the fruit not the seed. From Locke through Hume and Russell, British empiricism has validated knowledge by reference to its mode of origination; the pragmatic epistemology of American thought looks instead to the consequences of the idea, just as in American life (or in its ideology, at any rate) a man is judged by the fulfillment in his future, not by the promise in his antecedents. Not their source in God or Nature but their destination in man certifies human values.

This is to say that there are no value properties as such. There are no simple traits whose possession or lack is the mark of good and evil. A thing becomes of value by virtue of its status and function in ongoing behavior. Values are thought to be transcendental because every empirical property is just what it is, a brute fact, and its value is then imagined to extend into another dimension outside experience, religious or metaphysical. But its capacity to satisfy human desires, its delicacy in answering to human emotion, its readiness to respond to human volition—all this is also matter of fact and can be uncovered in experience.

Not that morality consists simply in the immediate satisfaction of desire! Such satisfactions are a necessary condition of value but not themselves sufficient. No act could be right which added only pain and suffering to the world, and which could not reasonably have been expected to do anything else. This morality belongs to the Devil. But an immediate experience of satisfaction cannot itself certify to morality, for life extends beyond the fleeting moment, and in the pursuit of any one value we must perforce put all our values at stake. Only long-range and comprehensive satisfactions suffice for moral judgment.

Science, too, must distinguish between reality and the momentary appearance to sense; yet it must relate all its truths to the world as sensed, while recognizing that what always and everywhere appears in a particular way really *is* as it appears to be. The proper contrast is not between appearance and reality, satisfaction and the good, but between a momentary appearance or a fleeting and passing satisfaction, and the enduring and comprehensive ones. In its own status every appearance is real, just as every felt good is genuinely good; the fool's paradise is just as heavenly—while it lasts. Our troubles come only when we move, as move we must, from what is here and now to what lies elsewhere. It is in this movement that we may find ourselves misguided; and only experience can be our guide.

Here, then, is a truly naturalistic ethics, one which bases values in the nature that flows through the channels of human sensibility. It is because of what we are, not what man is, that we are mindful of him; it is enough for human action that it attain a human good. Naturalism is the position that there is no other good; as C. I. Lewis put it, man's own experience is ultimately the only touchstone we have for what is good.[18] And it will serve.

On this theory, it is easy to see the importance for policy of a thorough-going knowledge of man's ways and works. But it is not the only theory which gives knowledge this place: the *philosophes* of the Enlightenment, the English utilitarians and French positivists, the "scientific" socialists of several varieties—all agreed in relying on experience to choose public policy. Given this agreement, differences in theory become secondary. There is a naturalistic core in every ethics which relies on experience for the recognition of what is good, even if it is not experience that *makes* it good. Even a religious ethic, if it is no longer involved with heavenly reward and punishment, must turn to naturalistic sanctions for its morality: the direct *experience* of good and bad consequences in this earthly life. We are all "empiricists" today, just as we are all "liberals"! But when there are differences on the level of moral practice, not just of ethical theory, the case is altered. Sooner or later the problem of relativism must be faced. Does naturalism bring us at last to the admission that the Russians are right in dismissing human rights as bourgeois values, and the knowledge on which their espousal rests as class science?

The centrality of man in modern political theory has raised the specter of relativism. "The fundamental difference between even ancient republican and modern democratic governments," Dewey has pointed out, "has its source in the substitution of human nature for cosmic nature as the foundation of politics." [19] While cosmic nature is single and constant, human nature is multiple and varied. It is one world, to be sure, but it is inhabited by many men, and they are not all alike. Class and culture do affect values, and within these large differences are the countless variations of lesser groupings and individual idiosyncrasies. When values become humanized, the way is opened for each man to play God, and the first act of infantile omnipotence is not to create but to destroy. Hence the moral nihilism of sophomoric rebellion, or the nihilism of the larger political rebellion expressed in that "critique of ideology" which dismisses as "propaganda" all political ideals—save the rebel's own.

But in the end these, too, must give way. If I must do God's work, it will after all remain undone. If my values are only in my think-so, they are no values at all. When a man mistakes himself for God he denies what is godly within him: the capacity to know and love the good in God's world—the world as it really is—and not just in the madhouse of his own mind. The sin is not in eating of the fruit of the tree of knowledge of good and evil, but in taking so little, and that from another's hand. It is the little learning, and that little once removed from our own direct experience of value, which is the dangerous thing.

The simple fact of moral experience is that what we judge is distinct from the fact of our judging it. Our judging, like all else we do, is conditioned by all that makes us what we are; but whether we have judged well or ill is not determined by those conditions. Science as a process of inquiry is as conditioned by society as are all other social practices and institutions. But this affects only what we believe, not what is true. We ask the questions in the language of our culture and prompted by our individual desires to know; but the answers are nature's. What is good for one man may not be so for another; this fact, however, is indifferent to what either man may think to be good, whether for himself or for the other. The principle of one man's meat holds true, but it does not undermine the objectivity of a dietetics grounded in physiology and a knowledge of the individual case. In short, relativism does not condemn us to subjectivity but frees us from it, for only when we have relativized the value judgment to the needs and circumstances of the human beings whose values are in question can the judgment become truly objective. We live each of us, not as we wish, but as we must, in the circumstances in which we find ourselves. Morality may impose upon us the duty to change these circumstances; it cannot become, nor would we have it become, any the less circumstantial.

This *objective relativism* contrasts markedly with the cultural relativism of a few decades ago. The comparative ethnology of the last century, in disclosing the astonishing variety in patterns of culture, was taken by many as providing a scientific warrant for moral subjectivism. Of course, it does no such thing; we cannot rationalize our failure to assume responsibility for our values by pointing out that they are not shared by the Kwakiutl. As a matter of fact, there is a wider commonalty of values than was at first supposed: all cultures impose taboos on murder and incest, for example, regulating in some fashion libidinal and aggressive impulses. More to the point is the recognition that each culture inhabits, in a very real sense, a world of its own—different in fact, and even more markedly different in what is taken to be fact. What is sound political morality in Massachusetts may not be so in Madagascar—and why should it! If it were, ignorance and error, in the one locale as in the other, would produce a show of disagreement without an underlying difference.

Conversely, there may be differences in value without disagreement, differences in taste which can be allowed for without invoking a margin for error. The Victorian ladies watching a tempestuous performance of *Antony and Cleopatra* were overheard to remark, "How different, how very different, from the home life of our own dear queen!" We need not fear that the awareness of other patterns forces upon us at once the burden of defending our own. Not every disagreement rests on a real difference, and not every difference involves a real conflict. As the world really becomes one, in fact and in the perspectives on it of the world's peoples, values also may be expected to be increasingly shared. And where they diverge, a larger value may lie in the divergence itself.

The Dualistic Code

I turn now from ethical theories to moral codes, from the foundations of moral judgment to its content. Ethics and morals are only loosely linked: the same values may be prized whether their warrant be from God, nature, or man; and the pursuit of different values may seek justification by appeal to the same ethics. Regardless of whether America bases its values on religion, on a metaphysics of natural rights, or on an empirical naturalism, what are its values?

At the very outset, we must face the stale charge of American "materialism," which over and over again has been pictured as excluding that life of the spirit in which religious, moral, esthetic, and intellectual values have their being. For some curious reason, classical imagery is usually invoked here: America is a new Carthage, sunk in barbaric sensuality; at the same time, it is a coarse and unfeeling Sparta, confronting the Athenian temper of a mellow European culture; or else it is another Rome, substituting engineering and military prowess for the glorious heritage of Greek civilization.

Whatever the metaphor, it is literalized in the platitudes describing America as an acquisitive society in which success is pursued at any price, worth measured by the dollar, and wealth made the basis of invidious distinction by expenditure for conspicuous consumption and waste. The indictment continues by charging that in America goods are thought to define the Good. All values are reduced to sales value, and even good will has a price put upon it. America is materialistic because above all else it prizes material objects; though its cars, refrigerators, and bathtubs are all that one could wish, Americans are incapable of genuine and deep satisfaction with them or with anything else. In short, in the course of the last half century Europe's image of America as "liberty lighting the world" has given way to the Hollywood stereotype of the poor little rich girl who owns everything and can enjoy nothing.

What is dangerous about this image is not merely the effect it has on the attitudes of other nations to us; it is even more dangerous because of the effect it has on our own self-image. Americans are pathetically prone to act out their fantasies. Nature imitates art—executives posture like men of distinction, lovers counterfeit the movie manner, statesmen groom themselves for television appearances and the covers of national weeklies. The danger in the myth of American materialism is that we will accept with enthusiasm—and naïveté—the role in which it casts us of the world's plumbers and policemen.

Properly understood, no myth is wholly mythical. The wildest dream fulfills some real wish, and plausibility demands a core of fact for every fantasy. We can recognize something of ourselves in the image Europeans project of us, which is no less ours because we can also see it so readily, if we choose, in those who are projecting it. In matters of religion, we must admit that the American Christmas is as much the concern of the chamber of commerce as of the church. As for morality, to the commandment "Honor thy father and mother" we have added the codicil "Say it with Flowers." The career of the fabulous Duveen makes it difficult to deny that art in America is a commodity, valued less for the esthetic experience it provides than for the prestige its ownership or even viewing confers. The works of the mind, if they are not laid to rest in a professional journal or a university press, must meet the exigencies of mass sales and the standards of book-club juries of selection. And nothing is more materialistic than the obscenities of the spirit with which in Southern California it is the custom to bury the dead.

Yet this core of truth in the falsehood of the caricature is not distinctively American. It is a by-product of civilizing agencies at work throughout the world. The deadening of the spirit and the corruption of the moral life with which America is charged is not an American invention; it is a concomitant, as Ortega y Gasset has persuasively argued, of mass man everywhere.[20] It is easy to present oneself as a member of the elite by sneering at mediocrity; none more loyal than those who denounce traitors! But the American middle class is no worse, though no better, than the middle class anywhere else. It is true that the push button and assembly line are destroying that sense of effort and sensitivity to materials essential to the creation and appreciation of works of art. But it is sheer prejudice that dismisses as untutored Yankee ingenuity the American contribution to the world's technology, while the contribution of other nations is supposed to attest to the high scientific level of their cultures.

But the defense that American "materialism" is largely a product of the conditions of life in the twentieth century is by no means an endorsement of the clichés which condemn twentieth-century civilization wholesale as a soulless technology. Without this technology, the soul might not have a body with which to live the life of the spirit. Lecky is a thousand times right when he declares that probably "the American inventor of the first anaesthetic has done more for the real happiness of mankind than all the moral philosophers from Socrates to Mill." [21] Care for the body, in America at any rate, has not been in the service of that hedonist sensuality which is so loathsome to the ministers of the spirit; the American ideal may be comfort, but it is certainly not pleasure—save perhaps in those backwashes of the South where the self-image of a decadent aristocracy is perpetuated. Technology has meant, for the most part, more food, clothing, and shelter—and must mean still more. European moralists must not be allowed to forget the wisdom of their own Aristotle: before a man can live well, he must be able to live.

Moreover, material achievement has made possible the widest access in history to the products of culture, and the widest sharing in its production and appreciation—in music, theater, letters, and the other arts. Behind the recurrent charge of Philistinism is perhaps no more than the fact, of which America can be proud, that we have no recognized leisure class of aesthetes and connoisseurs to serve as established arbiters of taste. And American standardization, after all, serves for society as a habit does for the individual: it may confine energies to a stifling routine, but it may also release them for creative effort.

America's material achievement needs no apology. What is indefensible is our failure to integrate the perspectives of this achievement with those in which our other values are defined and pursued. An age of material vigor is not necessarily backward in culture: it is usual to refer here to Pericles, Augustus, and the first Elizabeth. But what we have done is to dissociate values from their material embodiments, so that worth has become unreal, and much of our material reality worthless. This dissociation I call *cultural dualism*, and the value judgments it engenders the *dualistic code*.

Not every duality marks a dualism: there is after all a difference between an ideal end and the means realistically available for its attainment. But for the dualist this difference is thought to be absolute and irreconcilable, the distinction is drawn only to set the one against the other in far-reaching conflict, and the two are conceived as belonging to disparate metaphysical categories. The dualisms of spirit and matter, ideals and expediency, art and science, thought and action can be traced from Plato and Pauline Christianity through Descartes into modern times; in America today they are of enormous importance.

To the degree that ours is in very truth an acquisitive society, it is because of the separation we enforce between creation and ownership, between the instrumentality for the good life of what is acquired and the status mistaken for that life the mere acquisition confers. Work is unceasingly contrasted with leisure and few occupations pursued as a calling, so that occupational choices present the continuing dilemma—genuine only in the dualistic perspective—between prostituting a talent and burying it. One man is idealistic, another practical. Art is often treated, in Dewey's apt phrasing, as "the beauty parlor of civilization," moving out from the museums only to serve as irrelevant decoration. In short, beauty versus utility, thought versus action, theory versus practice—a Noah's ark of antediluvian pairings!

The situation with intellectual values is representative, and of particular importance in its own right for a political morality consisting in the best application of intelligence to the resources of political experience. The charge that America's worship of matter has cast mind into outer darkness is absurd. The United States today is undeniably a world center of scientific research and free scholarship. True, much of its creative effort is European in origin; but so is America itself. This great intellectual activity is now an integral part of the American scene. Our libraries, laboratories, and institutions of higher learning, taken all in all, rank with the best anywhere. European education is perhaps more intensive at an earlier age; but in my experience the difference disappears later on. And that so much education is here made available to so many is an intellectual as well as social gain which is not to be dismissed with cynical clichés about quantity and quality.

There is more basis to the criticism that intellectual effort in America is largely utilitarian in spirit, and that the mind is cultivated, not for its own sake, but in the service of government, industry, or individual ambition. The true and the beautiful are swallowed up in a utilitarian good. In many quarters philosophy and the humanities have taken up a defensive posture, seeking justification by claiming a contribution to science as "methodology" or to society as a way of filling the vacuum of increasing leisure. Yet the ideal of a "humanistic" education, when this is contrasted with a "technological" one, has been—as Dewey has tirelessly argued—not genuinely liberating, but a perpetuation of the standards of a leisure class, standards which are truly "materialistic" because they are derived from the status of those sufficiently wealthy to be spared the necessity of doing anything useful.

What remains true is that in America there is a continuing strain of anti-intellectualism, a persistent dislike and distrust of ideas and the men who live for them, possibly no stronger than in the past, but politically more influential. If any attitude be "un-American" this one is, for the Republic was founded by men of ideas who prized the works of the mind. Jefferson wished to be remembered as the founder of the University of Virginia; a college presidency today is a step to higher things, and too marked a literacy is a serious political handicap. It is not political partisanship to recognize that in America the capacities of the human mind often evoke fear rather than pride and hope—fear not just of the physical destructiveness they might engender, but also of the dissolution they may bring about of traditional patterns presumed to be too sickly to resist the germ of an idea.

For in this perspective, "ideas" are equated with "ideologies," ideas about "social" institutions identified with "socialism." Nor is this only a semantic blunder of illiteracy. The National Science Foundation encourages the study of "human resources" but not of "social science"—or it would encounter Congressional opposition. And a distinguished man of letters recently declared in a well-received book on American life that "our absence of ideas, the exclusion of ideas from American political life, gives us a superior kind of public morality," for ideas are the stuff of ideology, and ideology in turn makes for enforced and undemocratic unity.[22] I hope I have misunderstood him. But our hysterical fears of "subversive scientists" are expressed in actions that cannot be misunderstood. Perhaps these fears give ground, after all, for insisting that it is we who represent Athens and Europe, Sparta; for it is here that Socrates might have been put on trial for his security clearance.

The problems of military security are special, to be sure; but what is involved is the general question of the social and political role of ideas.

I am not arguing for the privileges of a caste of "intellectuals"; I am arguing against the emasculation of intellect which condemns it to social sterility. It is hard to believe today that so shrewd an observer as Bryce was at one time able to report that in America "intellectual eminence . . . is more admired and respected than in Europe." [23] In the last quarter-century, since the early days of the New Deal and its "brain trust," intellectual eminence, whatever admiration it has commanded, has occupied a shifting and uneasy place in government. The makers of policy are increasingly recruited from business, finance, and industry, less and less from science, art, or education; the occasional exceptions are markedly more infrequent than their counterparts in Europe. There are in government, of course, considerable numbers of "symbol specialists" (as they are called by contemporary analysts of "elite structures")— which is to say: lawyers, publicists, and the like. The question, however, is not one of facility with words but with the ideas for which words are instruments. From this point of view, the philosopher Sri Radhakrishnan, the Vice President of India, provides almost a symbolic contrast with some of our own. We may not need to import the wisdom of the East; but we need desperately the domestic article.

I do not mean to say that contemporary anti-intellectualism is something new in American life. There has always been a civil war on this front, and the strategic position of the man of ideas is no worse today than it has been on several occasions in the past. Western agrarianism, with its hostility to intellection, has been as much a part of American politics as the high culture of New England. The fact is that the American attitude toward intellectuals has always been ambivalent. The problem becomes acute only when the chronic inner conflict is externalized; and what is then crucial is the character of the culturally acceptable ways of resolving the conflict. What I am protesting is the tendency to seek such resolutions by a partition of sovereignty between the thinkers and doers. This is why I speak of our code as dualistic: not that we reject the life of the mind but that we insulate it from the world of action. In Santayana's words, the dualism consists in "that separation which is so characteristic of America between things intellectual, which remain wrapped in a feminine veil and, as it were, under glass, and the rough business and passions of life." [24] Things intellectual we confine either to the selection of appropriate means—the myth of scientific neutralism—

or else to the purely verbal specification of abstract ends too remote to have any effect on policy. In our important choices, we largely disregard the intelligent habits, skills, and attitudes so effectively cultivated within the scientific enterprise. The dangers of such separatism are not just those of an amoral intellectuality, but even more those of an unintelligent, unrealistic morality. As it has been from the beginning, we might be able to deal with the scoundrels—if only we are not first destroyed by the fools.

What is foolish is the simple-minded morality which is indifferent to mere matters of fact, the thoughtlessness of Shaw's Sergius in *Arms and the Man* who with flashing saber leads a cavalry charge against a battery of machine guns. What sublime heroism! Yes, and what disastrous stupidity! There is no question that Americans are idealists: we have Wilson's word for it that "America is the only idealist nation in the world." [25] But it is idealism of a peculiarly adolescent kind—unyielding, unrealistic, otherworldly—in a word, romantic. It starts out, not from where we are, but from where we *would* be, if only we had the making of the world in our own hands; and it ends where it should begin. We undertake to bring to their senses whole nations, but not the necessary majority of the United States Senate. And what then! We may lose the good fight, but it will be well fought, and to the very end we will keep— our white plume. Alas for these childhood dreams of glory!

Such romantic idealism has played a considerable part in American reform movements and in American political life generally. "Sometimes people call me an idealist," Wilson says again. "Well, that is the way I know I am an American." [26] And he is right. Domestically, the idealist's image of himself has been that of a St. George attacking the dragons of Big Business, Crooked Politics, and Vested Interests. The familiar cycle of municipal reform in the United States documents in full both the ideal impulse and its realistic failure. In foreign affairs we picture ourselves as actuated only by moral considerations, while other nations go whoring after the false gods of their own self-interest. "In each of the two world wars," Laski comments, "American participation has seemed to some millions of its citizens not a necessary policy of self-defence, but a genuine act of charity, in which the president and Congress were deliberately casting their vote for right against wrong." [27] More recently, our policy in the Middle East has been presented to the world as the path of international righteousness from which our friends, alas, have strayed. But we will teach them self-denial for the sake of moral ideals.

This is as far as the idealist goes in his analysis of the moral problem: moral conflict is always between duty and desire, and morality stands unequivocally on the side of duty. For the adolescent, perhaps, this analysis may have elements of realism: his maturation rests on his coming to terms with powerful impulses. But in the world of men, such formulations are superficial and simplistic. There are conflicts among desires and among duties as well as between them. The problem is not how to carry out an easily recognizable idealistic policy, but how to reconcile conflicting ideals in a concrete context of their incompatibility, how to satisfy conflicting desires in circumstances that threaten to frustrate one or another of them. These are the conflicts which make a situation realistically problematic; and with regard to these, moralizing idealism is silent. It has recourse instead to a rhythm of sin and repentance, a sporadic self-righteousness which leaves us afterwards free to sin again. We alternate between a resolute response to the call of duty, until we win the war, and a return to the free indulgence of desire, until we lose the peace.

Here we come to the core of the dualistic code. It formulates conflicts as lying always between moral ends and immoral means. Success, it enjoins, must never be purchased at the expense of principles—which is to say that principles have nothing to do with realistic possibilities of attaining projected ends. In consequence, ethereal moral losses are counterposed to concrete though immoral gains; the resultant imbalance suprises no one but the dualistic idealist himself. When ideals are so conceived that in their very nature they stand opposed to expediency, it is foreordained which will give way. Necessity knows no law, and least of all a moral law. Dualism, in divorcing fact and value, seeks to place morality above necessity, and thereby puts it out of reach altogether of action enmeshed in causal necessitation.

The editors of an influential American magazine proclaim to other nations that we have learned how to have the best of both worlds: "Americans live on two planes at once—the practical and the ideal. The conflicts created by this ambivalent existence, which worry other people so much that they often feel constrained to reject one plane or the other, bother the American scarcely at all." [28] Might we not feel constrained instead to overcome the gulf between these two planes? No man, not even an American, can serve two masters. If we are not bothered it is because we have fragmented our lives, institutionally and individually, to accommodate both. We look to practicality in business and politics, and to the realm of the ideal in religion and morality. As businessman, scientist, politician, I have one responsibility; as father, husband, citizen, another. It is all a question of the role I am to play. And a play of shadows is what the pursuit of ideals then becomes, especially in the context of public policy. "Do-gooder," "world-improver," "reformer," Riesman perceptively observes, are "terms of contempt or friendly dismissal: to want to 'do good' in politics is obviously to be naive"[29] —as it must be, if we act naively. And so the final outcome is cynicism and disillusionment. But to be disillusioned there is one thing necessary—that we first be victims of illusion.

VULGAR PRAGMATISM

America has often been charged with being a nation of opportunists— a half-truth which ignores the important element of idealism in American life. But the dualistic code does give ground for the charge up to a point. When ideals are confined to the determination of ultimate ends, "practicality" remains the only standard for the choice of proximate means. But action is an unending sequence of such proximate choices; we touch the ultimate only in death. The core of truth in the charge that America worships success lies in this bent of the man of affairs: not that for him only success counts, but that he looks to it for the opportunity *afterwards* to apply it to ideal ends. The revised American version is: Seek ye the kingdom of this earth; and all these godly things shall be added unto you.

It is useless to pretend that we do not largely accept success on its own terms: only the bankrupt has engaged in sharp practices, just as only the defeated candidate was guilty of dirty politics. Virtue always triumphs when triumph is the supreme virtue, and the triumphant the recognized arbiters of public morals. The history of the great American fortunes is ethically less interesting for the immoralities of their acquisition than for the moral force they were able to exert when acquired. Some recent distinguished political careers bring this documentation up to date. Yet what is often overlooked in this condemnation is that success is rarely in American life an end in itself. It is pursued, in a pathetic dependency on social acceptance, not for pleasure or power, but for admiration, love, and even self-respect.

In all this there is nothing of the philosophical pragmatism of Peirce, James, and Dewey, but only a vulgarized caricature. The emphasis on what works was meant by them as an insistence on the instrumentality of ideas for the enrichment of immediate experience. This is not the place to examine the persistent European misunderstandings of American pragmatism, but it is tiresome to have even Americans rationalize expediencies as a healthy "pragmatism," in the way in which a libertine might lean on Freud. Pragmatism is no more the working philosophy of America than the teachings of Jesus are its working religion. When Russell characterizes pragmatism as the philosophy of American business it is hard to say which of the two he has more seriously misunderstood. (Dewey was once moved to reply to this characterization with the remark that one might with equal justice attribute Cartesian dualism 'ɔ the Gallic propensity for keeping a mistress as well as a wife—to which Russell rejoined, "Precisely!")

What cannot be denied is that there is something in pragmatism which lends itself to this vulgarization. An ethics which demands only the continuing application of intelligence to the problems of men without recourse to principles or powers outside experience does not invite spectacular acts of courage and devotion. It calls rather for that quiet heroism which so easily gives way, as was recognized long ago, to a quiet desperation. But there is nothing in pragmatism of the frame of mind for which the paradigm of the pragmatic lies in meeting a payroll or winning an election.

The issue here is not one of philosophical exegesis; what is at stake is not the correctness of a philosophical interpretation, but the morality of a pattern of action. In holding up the ideal of success, vulgar pragmatism does not ground values in existence, but takes as valuable whatever is existent. The test of success is essentially the same as the test of survival applied in "social Darwinism." What survives is the fittest—the fittest, of course, to survive; but competitive success is taken to be at once the sign and the substance of worth. This is the morality of the trial by combat, with the God who ensures that the right will prevail replaced by natural forces. When success is its own justification, the moral order is reduced to a purely historical one—retrospective, as in Hegel's "whatever is, is right," or prospective, as in the fascist or communist Wave of the Future. To be sure, a good which cannot be made to work is no good at all to us; but the Devil also has his triumphs, and when we have hit upon what works, the question still remains: whose work have we done?

To the ideal of success vulgar pragmatism also adds the ideal of efficiency, the most economic adaptation of available means to given ends. The vulgarization lies in the narrowness with which both means and ends are conceived. Economy implies the conservation of some values whose expenditure is required to achieve others. It becomes a false economy, a mere show of efficiency, when important values are left out of the accounting. This is the usual fate of the so-called human values which are the domain of morality. It characterizes the efficiency on which the fascist states prided themselves: the trains to the gas chambers ran on schedule.

In America efficiency is the fetish of the business world, and the operation of a business the model for politics and personal life. The promise of a business administration is almost irresistible to the American electorate, and a balanced budget is the Holy Grail of presidential Galahads. That the budgeting for a state rests on wholly different economic considerations than that for a private enterprise is a subtlety left to the long hairs of functional finance. The plain man will stand for no nonsense: he wants the most for his money. And the prudent politician will convince him that that is what he is getting.

In personal life this is the morality of double-entry bookkeeping. For such a morality, honesty is a matter of policy, generosity is good business, friendship pays off. We have risen above the nadir of a few decades ago when the Man of Sorrows was presented in a best seller as a cheerfully successful Rotarian. But efficiency remains a compelling ideal. I have forgotten which of the English utilitarians it was who chose his wife by listing in order of desirability all the eligible women of his acquaintance and proposing down the list until he was accepted. Such a man in America today could be a member of any Team in the country, and would even be admired for the sureness of his taste. Sense and sensibility are one. The same writer who found moral values in the exclusion of ideas from our political life finds aesthetic values in the standard of efficiency: "Americans' lust for possessions satisfies not a physical, but a metaphysical need. The pleasure is in having the instrument that works, in fitness. Efficiency is after all an artistic criterion—economy of matter and sufficiency of form." [30] No doubt it is this artistry which is responsible for the overpowering economy of matter and sufficiency of form in the American automobile.

There is no gainsaying the real efficiency achieved in American technology, and no intention here to derogate its value. The question is whether morality itself is a branch of technology. Vulgar pragmatism here unites with another important stream of contemporary American life: that misplaced and misconceived admiration of science aptly called *scientism*. Pragmatism yields to no philosophy in its emphasis on the significance of science for human affairs. But for it, science is a method—a temper of mind and a habit of action. Scientism identifies science with transitory results taken to be definitive and, even more, with special instruments and techniques taken to be the method itself.

Prominent among these are the procedures of quantification. The alleged American worship of bigness is itself a victim of European exaggeration; but Americans do attach excessive importance to exactitude. Nothing is so real as a measurable quantity. And if what is measured is good, the more the better. Under the impact of scientism, formation of policy is unduly influenced by considerations of dollars, votes, units of production; the data of a problem are those things that can be summarized in tables to appear in memoranda prepared by the experts. We can sympathize with that subject of Kinsey's who complained bitterly of the deflation of his masculine ego: "No matter what I told him, he just looked me straight in the eye and asked, 'How many times?'" Love is dealt with as sex and sex as ejaculation. Here at last we have something we can count. It would be well if we could measure the extent to which such reductionism affects our thinking on problems of health, education, housing, and employment—to say nothing of the mysteries in the trinity of peace, prosperity, and progress.

Applied social science can point to impressive success in such fields as marketing, personnel selection, and even labor relations. But there is often more impressiveness than success. If government suffers from the disease of bureaucracy, the bureaucrat himself is infected with scientism. Decisions are not the product of judgment and imagination, prudence and courage, but of surveys, questionnaires, graphs, and charts, of endless

memoranda and reports, and, at last, of studies by special commissions just below the august policy-making level. One would almost suppose that to be scientific means not to think at all: the gadget, in the hands of the proper expert, will do it for us.

But this travesty of science is paralyzed in the face of imponderables, and for the morality of public policy the imponderables are everything. It is for just this reason that the brave new worlds of Huxley and Orwell are so morally repugnant. In them, not the scientific but the scientistic treatment of man has been carried to its conclusion: human engineering is at last totally and hideously efficient, without the saving absurdities of Chaplin's *Modern Times* or René Claire's *A nous la liberté*. The standard of efficiency leads inexorably to the treatment of man as a means, one among others. And because morality must take man as an end in himself, the moral impulse in American life is often expressed as a generalized hostility to science and all its works. Such admiration as the scientist receives is generously compounded with fear and distrust. In the end, scientism does not serve the cause of science, but enlists against science all the agencies of morality, within the self and in social institutions. And morality it condemns to be molded only by tradition, prejudice, and sentimentality.

What is called the "pragmatic" temper of the American mind is thus very far from pragmatic, however plausibly it is rationalized as the "scientific" treatment of our problems. It is efficient only if we do not count the cost, successful only in attaining the values we have fixed upon beforehand, not those in fact implicated in our actions. To simplify choices we isolate ends, confident in our innocence that what we have put asunder God will not join together. In any situation we suppose only one value to be at stake; what is essential in the light of the end we have in view becomes the essence of the matter in very truth, and the essence, in turn, not the heart but the whole. And on the unanticipated consequences of action morality goes aground. To the childish mind the adult is only more successful, more efficient, in the pursuit of childish things.

We are at war? Who does not know that the aim of war is victory! Its object, then, can be nothing less than unconditional surrender. To achieve that object all effort must be bent: total war for total victory. On the American banner is inscribed not "Exclesior!" but "Eccessivo!" More and still more—everything for victory, only the victory! This is the breathless virility Europeans mistake for mere braggadocio. But, for all that, it is a grievous fault, and grievously do we answer for it: in World War I, the hysterical renunciation of the German language, German poetry, German music; in World War II, the inhumanities of the uprooting of the Japanese from the West Coast, to say nothing of the atom bomb; and in the Cold War, the immolation of friendship, faith, and even family—all in the name of loyalty. Loyalty to what? to values genuine in themselves, but pitiable things when torn loose from the body of living democracy.

Perhaps, after all, it is the American division of labor, and not American vigor, which must bear the blame. The expert on military strategy or foreign affairs, on the farm problem or labor relations, is just that and nothing more; in government an expert on morals would be an archaic absurdity. In arriving at policy, we calculate with precision half the distance, and content ourselves with a casual guess at the rest—and it is usually the second half which is exactly measured. The philosophy of American decision making is not pragmatism but utilitarianism, in the spirit of Dewey's characterization of the latter as "an intricate calculus of remote, inaccessible and indeterminate results." I propose to call this isolation of value the utilitarian fallacy: the appraisal of means by calculation of their effects on partial and perhaps secondary ends.

It is a cruel misunderstanding to charge Americans with immorality. Few peoples are more scrupulously righteous than we, when we recognize an issue as moral. But how seldom we recognize it! Our approach to the day-to-day decisions of government is largely utilitarian in the sense I have just given it. Ethics is thought to bear on policy, not from within, but only at the edges. Our conception of political morality is legalistic: we usually suppose morality to be threatened only when the law is violated. For the mass of the citizenry, policy raises moral issues only when its adoption or administration involves bribery, corruption, or venality. If from the wholly legal workings of policy patent injustices result, we suppose morality to be served by acts of philanthropy or executive clemency. Morality demands mitigation of effects; correction of causes is not the domain of morals, but of hardheaded practicality.

Alas, morality of this kind is a luxury product and will give way whenever we can no longer afford the philanthropies. It is easy for the rich to be generous and the powerful forgiving. "Does Job fear God for nought?

Have You not made a hedge about him, and about his house, and about all that he has, on every side? You have blessed the work of his hands, and his possessions are increased in the land." [31] What happens now that the hedge about us has given way? One recourse still remains. Morality is still important as the basis of morale: our own, our friends', and the morale of neutrals whose friendship is to be won by our show of morality. Today, desegregation is as often urged for its effect on neutralist Asiatics as on Americans themselves. Not our own ideals but someone else's idealizations become morally decisive.

This transformation of morality to morale accords well with the tough-mindedness on which American "pragmatism," so called, prides itself. For morality appears to many Americans as properly a feminine pre-occupation, like elementary schoolteaching, social welfare work, or indeed any serious cultivation of intellectual and aesthetic values. De Tocqueville had already noted that morals are "the work of women"; [32] and various surveys, in this country and abroad, have shown that it is women who are especially concerned with morality in politics—at least in the sense in which this involves such matters as liquor, gambling, and political corruption.[33] Whether the greater interest of women in these questions relates, as has been suggested, to their greater participation in religious activities, or has some other basis—independent of the facts—the image of morality as feminine is well established in American life.

In these terms, the appeal to morality in politics faces the deep-rooted resistance of anxiety as to one's masculinity. To be a man is to be successful, efficient, even ruthless; sympathy, gentleness, and consideration are restraints imposed by the tender sensibilities of woman. A man, in short, is thought to prove his masculinity by his capacity of aggression, not for love; but it is love that morality calls for. Thus moral impulses find themselves blocked, as generosity, for instance, is inhibited by the fear of being shown up as a sucker. Americans are often more deeply motivated by moral considerations than they themselves pretend to be: we may rationalize our virtues even more than our vices. Our "pragmatism" may be a pretense to preserve the masculine ego.

Thus morality is first feminized, then rejected. In politics, to be conspicuously moral is to be not good but goody-goody: a boy scout, a Sunday school teacher—in a word, unmanly. The political leader must above all never be naive or a soft touch. A streak of femininity is tolerated and—by the female electorate—even welcomed: he may be gentle with children, animals, and Mother. But he may not under any circumstances go soft on matters of policy. Here he must be unwaveringly hardheaded, hard-boiled, hard to get, and even harder to get around. I am tempted to conclude that in the perspectives of vulgar pragmatism, the affairs of the country would be in the best hands if we could turn them over to a "private eye."

Moral Absolutism

American morality is largely a morality of principle—so much so that we may find it hard to imagine that a morality could be anything else. We are self-consciously moral; to do what comes naturally is to be wicked or, at best, irresponsible. Though our idealism is romantic, we have rejected the romanticism of natural innocence, with its belief that we can do right by instinct if this is uncorrupted by civilized sophistication. We are too divided within ourselves to be able to trust our native impulses. We let conscience be our guide, but only because conscience rests on moral principles. Our moral philosophy has a strongly Platonist cast: generalized abstractions come first. The particularities of concrete choices do not justify the principles but are justified by them. The logic of morals is deductive; facts, not values, are arrived at inductively.

Such an appeal to principle has several important contributions to make to morality. To start with, it precludes that unexamined life which Socrates condemned as not worth living. If decisions are to be justified by principles, they must be preceded by reflective appraisals of alternatives. Principled action, whatever its shortcomings, is not heedless, makeshift, or arbitrary. As moralists, Americans are likely to feel that life is real and earnest; and while this often imposes on our morality a leaden solemnity and even grimness, it saves us from the emptiness of pure caprice and the deadly necessities of meaningless routine.

What is more, principled action deepens the significance of personal decisions by basing them on universalized standards. The principle will not countenance the irrelevancy that my choice is, after all, mine. If an act is not obligatory on all men in my position it is not an obligation on me; and I have no moral right which would not belong equally to any other man situated as I am. Kant, the superlative exponent of the ethics of principle, counters the moral aloneness of the autonomous will by the shared rationality of the principles to which that will subjects itself.

To act on principle is to universalize action in another dimension: not only from person to person but also from case to case. It is to decide on the basis of what is usually involved, on the outcome in the long run, in general. To appeal to "the principle of the thing" is to take the special instance as representative of a class; whatever the outcome in *this* instance, what is decisive is the consequence that would follow if the whole class were to be treated on the basis of the principle in question. Principles thus provide an element of conservatism in action, binding each case as it arises to patterns already established as preserving the values sought for. Moral values disclosed by the Prophets are sustained by the Law; legal institutions perform this function of conservation for societal values. But, in both cases, the forces of conservatism may be so great as to stifle the creative morality, the transvaluation of values, continuously called for in a changing world. In science, too, the generalizations we designate "laws" do not legislate for nature, but set down conditions new truths must meet to conserve the facts accommodated by the old.

What principled action preserves in the individual we call character, the integrity that unifies the personality as it faces successive moral decisions. The betrayal of principle in any decision is morally subversive, for action leaves its residue in habit, and habit in character. The generality of the principle by which action is to be guided answers to this generalizing tendency in action itself. The moral collapse of character is not a single dramatic event, like the schoolboy's fall of Rome, but a gradual corrosion of the mainsprings of action. The barbarian is first a hired guardian of the frontier, then a general of the army; and at last the emperor himself is no longer a Roman.

Choices can thus find justification in principles. To act on principle is to act in moral self-defense. Or, rather, it is to act in defense of the wished-for self, the self in the making. American insistence on principle is a species of moral ambition, a determination to live up to our own ego ideal. Virtue, to be sure, cannot be forced; even its nurture is attended by the sin of spiritual pride. Yet the lure of the ideal, to be effective in action, must be joined by some drive within the personality. What begins as a role to be played may in the end define the character itself, as in Max Beerbohm's fable of the Happy Hypocrite. That the

American appeal to principle may be insincere signifies nothing; the moment of truth transpires in action. It is here that our morality of principle may be found wanting.

American principles are likely to concern themselves with ultimates, while action is a matter always of the next step. Principles define inherent values, but the assessment of instrumental values leads to concrete choices. A code of principles is not a map of action but a guidebook for ultimate destinations. Thereby it serves the armchair traveler and provides an escape from responsible commitment to the decisions actually before him. That American folk hero, the henpecked husband, boasts that in his household he makes the important decisions: his wife selects his job, his house, his children's schools; he has sole authority on questions of foreign policy, presidential candidates, and nuclear tests. The idlers of Pershing Square and Columbus Circle discuss only the largest issues: "Do you believe in God?—take either side!" The morality of principle, as Kant saw, turns on motives, not consequences; thus a debate on principles offers the incomparable advantage of irresponsibility. Weber points out: "There is an abysmal contrast between conduct that follows the maxim of an ethic of ultimate ends—that is, in religious terms, 'The Christian does rightly and leaves the results with the Lord'—and conduct that follows the maxim of an ethic of responsibility, in which case one has to give an account of the foreseeable results of one's action." [34] The man of principle is, to be sure, morally invulnerable; but for a reason that also makes him politically irresponsible.

The ultimates of principle ignore not only consequences but also conditions. Ideals are in the nature of things abstract; everything concrete is actual. Principles necessarily abstract, therefore, from the particular conditions in terms of which alone ideals can be actualized. Specifically, they are likely to localize moral problems in the character of the individual, without regard to societal pressures and possibilities. This error Laski has called "the fallacy of abstraction," and finds it "a central element in Americanism." "The individual is not seen in his context as a member of a particular society at a particular time; he is seen as an individual standing outside society who can by an act of will, sometimes called faith, assure his own regeneration." [35] Real problems are thus given unreal formulations which substitute artificial questions of principle for the genuine issues of the specific circumstances. Such questions resemble the sophomoric riddles of moral choice. I am in a boat with my wife and my mother; it capsizes; whom do I save? Alas, I cannot swim! How would I spend a million dollars? That depends on how I get it; perhaps the wisest course would be to set aside half for my legal defense. Such childishness is given a sophisticated cover in political debate; but at bottom—may I say, "in principle"?—the error is the same. What is relevant to moral choice is treated as settled beforehand, and so tacitly assumed; but just this is the real issue.

Too often the statement of the moral problem is mistaken for its solution. The underlying assumption is that we already know all the answers to our moral problems. Man, it is said over and over again, "knows thoroughly well what moral conduct is, has known for thousands of years." [36] The task, then, is thought to be only one of applying this knowledge— that is, of getting others to do so, for, of course, those who support my policies have already applied it. In this perspective, political morality is essentially a matter of police action; it calls for rigorous enforcement of the law, not wisdom in legislating it. Such wisdom has already been provided—by Moses and Solon, by the fathers of the church and of our country. And if enforcement itself raises problems, we do not ask whether something might be wrong with the law. It is taken for granted in America that morality is unpleasant and unpopular, in accord with the miscalled "Puritanism" of American ethics.

This fantastic belief in the sufficiency of our moral knowledge is sustained by the abstractness of our principles. Surely we have been shown what the Lord requires of us: that we seek justice, love mercy, and walk humbly with our God. How we are to do these things is no longer, we imagine, a moral question but a matter of expediencies. And thus in the name of justice and mercy we may in all humility make secure our supply of Middle Eastern oil. In our foreign policy we presuppose what it is the task of moral action to create: a real community of men and nations which can give content and direction to the moral obligations of the members of that community.

The abstractness of principles thus makes them as useful politically as they are useless morally. The image of morality can be preserved in the abstraction while expediencies govern concrete choices. In this way "natural rights" have been used to resist the real extension of rights in welfare legislation, just as today restrictive clauses and covenants take refuge in the morality of "the principle of free choice of associations." We can enjoy the satire in Orwell's "All men are equal, but some are more equal than others"; but we fail to see through our own rationalizations. In a democracy these have a particularly important function: the politician seeks the widest possible support and avoids positions so definite as to alienate part of his constituency. Popularity requires that he take his stand on the virtues of the American Home and the viciousness of Foreign Aggression. The most partisan critic of our policy makers cannot accuse them of favoring Sin.

Policy itself becomes in a real sense unprincipled when it fails to recognize the contextualism of moral laws. For these, like scientific generalizations, have their conditions and limits, not exhaustively formulable in additional generalizations, but requiring operational anchorage in the particular case. No one has seen this more clearly than Aristotle in his devastating attack on Plato's Idea of the Good. "I am at a loss to know how the weaver or the carpenter would be furthered in his art by a knowledge of this absolute good, or how a man would be rendered more able to heal the sick or to command an army by contemplation of the pure form or idea. For it seems to me that the physician does not even seek for health in this abstract way, but seeks for the health of man, or rather of some particular man, for it is individuals that he seeks to heal." [37] With characteristic restraint Aristotle concludes, "In discussions on subjects of moral action, universal statements are apt to be too vague, but particular ones are more consistent with truth; for actions are conversant with particulars; and it is necessary that the statements should agree with these." [38]

Generalizations have their place in moral reflection, and we cannot generalize without abstracting from the differences which individuate particulars. But to the empirical temper, generalizations depend on the individual case. A particular decision is not right because it accords with principle; the principle is valid only as it is warranted by the rightness of the particular decisions it encompasses. In scientific inquiry an established law may be used to discredit an alleged fact incompatible with it; but in the end the law must be verified by such allegations or lose its empirical standing altogether. In the same way, the principles which Americans regard as the backbone of character are not wholly without moral application. But character itself must be capable of growth. Americans speak always of "building" character, as though once erected it need only be periodically strengthened but never be redesigned to meet the challenge of new situations. It is this point of view that I call our moral absolutism.

The rigidity of character is expressed politically in a fixation on policies successful in the past, without regard to present conditions, which are tacitly assumed to have remained as they always were. Every neurotic pattern is realistic in relation to some situation which once was actually experienced, in fact or symbol. The core of the pathology is a disturbance of memory—not that the past is forgotten, but that action is determined by a remembrance which is mistaken for a present perception. Moral rigidity is easily rationalized by an appeal to the permanence of fixed principles. Conversely, such changes as occur in the conceptions of good and evil are presented as nothing more than the application of the old principles to new situations. Americans are as reluctant to recognize that new principles might be called for as Communists are to admit the reality of a change in party line. Our periodic return in politics to the paths of righteousness is uncommonly like the Communist rescue of Marxist-Leninism from betrayal by crypto-fascist traitors.

The notorious American worship of novelty is thus at best a superficial truth. Just as every drunk argues his sobriety, every conservative prides himself on being forward looking, and in both cases the self-image betrays the reality. America is essentially a conservative nation, and nowhere more than in its morality. What the world knows as "modern" is French art, German science, Swedish design. Americans prize novelty of expression but not of substance—her dress must be in the mode, but the little woman would look good in anything! We are married to our morality, and stick to our principles until death do us part. "When [Americans] have accepted a principle," Bryce observes, "they do not shrink from applying it 'right through,' however disagreeable in particular cases some of the results may be. . . . They prefer certainty and uniformity to the advantages which might occasionally be gained by deviation." [39]

Moral absolutism also expresses itself in treating its values as unconditional. The morality of "my country right or wrong" is not altogether groundless. Loyalty knows no reasons, and love is not love which alters when it alteration finds. Yet some moral limits are surely presupposed by the morality of loyalty and love. Absolutism sweeps these limits aside or, rather, is blind to their existence. In defense of loyalty we have attacked public men for sticking by their friends, private citizens for insisting on their constitutional rights, and reformed sinners for exhibiting the virtues of forbearance and Christian charity. Even if a man be wrong in refusing to name his suspect associates, surely moral issues must be resolved before he can be flatly judged wrong. Absolutism does not disentangle these issues but cuts through them. It goes further and, like Heaven itself, rejoices more in the repentant sinner than in the righteous man whom it suspects of sins yet to come.

That no values are absolute means only that conditions and consequences are always relevant to our appraisals of them. Every end is also a means: it is the utilitarian fallacy all over again to suppose that a value can be isolated from the matrix of its causes and effects. Would we have a Russian act on the morality of "my country right or wrong"? Is my loyalty an unquestionable virtue and his a damnable fault, the patriotism of my party an absolute good and the patriotism of the opposition the refuge of scoundrels? If conditions must be met in the one case, why not in the other? God Himself looked upon His creation before He pronounced it good.

Absolute values are likely to be extremist as well as unconditional. Our morality is sharply etched in black and white. Its paradigm is the TV western where virtues are all on one side, vices all on the other, and the distinction between the two easily apparent even to a child. And the distinction is entirely a question of character, not of specific acts and their consequences. These signify only as expressions of character: the villain is immediately recognizable because he is not clean shaven and beats his horse. It is this childish morality which we often project onto the political scene, and especially in our foreign relations. Its outcome is a continuing sense of betrayal by our friends and bewilderment by our enemies, as the former reveal human failings and the latter some qualities of human decency. And as for ourselves, anything less than moral superlatives borders on subversion. Justice Holmes recognized this immaturity when he criticized the absolutism of the doctrine of natural law: "It is not enough for the knight of romance that you agree that his lady is a nice girl—if you do not admit that she is the best God ever made or will make you must fight." [40] In sum, the absolutist forgets too easily that even a saint falls short of the Godhead, and even Satan, though fallen, is a fallen angel.

Absolutistic—that is to say, unconditional, unqualified, unquestioned. American morality is likely to be presented as indubitably certain; it follows the Cartesian logic of the incorrigible premise. If our premises are unsure, how can we have confidence in our conclusions? We must begin with what we cannot doubt, or the cancer of skepticism will prove fatal at last. Thus moral principles are rarely thought of as hypotheses, for this would make them "merely" hypothetical. To say that they are warranted in the light of all the evidence we have is to admit that as experience grows, new evidence may call for their reappraisal and even— who can say?—their rejection. But then what would be left for our guidance? If the stars in the heavens are no longer fixed, by what shall we set our course?

In terms of this logic we are strongly motivated to treat our values as beyond question, lest we be left without an answer. "To the good American," Santayana says, "many subjects are sacred: sex is sacred, business is sacred, America is sacred, Masonic lodges and college clubs are sacred. This feeling grows out of the good opinion he wishes to have of these things, and serves to maintain it. If he did not regard all these things as sacred he might come to doubt sometimes if they were wholly good." [41] It is this which gives the dogmatic cast to American morality. Dogmatism does not consist just in the bareness of our affirmation: we cannot forever be giving grounds for all we assert. What is dogmatic is the refusal to countenance questions, the frame of mind which regards doubt as foolish and even wicked. In many quarters today our accepted values are beyond discussion—either because, like labor relations, they are too "controversial," or because, like the relations between the sexes, they are too sacred for controversy. An absolutistic morality is always accompanied by an absolute authority, a chaperone to preserve inviolate its fragile virtue. This accords well with the current distrust of the freely questioning intellect which we have already noted. Authority does not speak as frankly today as did the seventeenth-century governor of Virginia who declared, "Thank God, there are no free schools or printing; . . . for learning has brought disobedience and heresy . . . into the world, and printing has divulged them. . . . God keep us from both." [42] The words sound harsh to modern ears; but few in America today do not recognize the tune.

True, disrespect for authority is also an American tradition, stemming from our Revolution, our ideology of distrust of government, the spirit of the frontier, and the individualism expressed throughout our culture patterns. Yet freedom from authority is not easily come by, and what is won by one generation cannot easily be handed down to the next. American reliance on conscience and the personal moral sense provides an inviting domain for the sovereignty of an introjected authority, which may rule even more tyrannically than the despots alien to the self. Since Freud, the destructive potentialities of conscience—the despotisms of the ideal—have been widely recognized. Erich Fromm and others have directed attention to the powerful anonymous authority which finds expression in the mass media and elsewhere in our conformist culture. As a result of its working, the immature personality, escaping from a dreadful freedom, may insist on subservience to principle with the compulsiveness of a child's anxiety over bedtime rituals. There is even a danger that psychiatry in its turn will be elevated into a new moral authority; it is easier for the slave to change masters than to achieve emancipation.

An absolutistic morality cannot take hold on democratic politics, for politics in a democracy is essentially pluralistic, tolerant, compromising. In the absolutistic perspective moral intolerance is a virtue and even a duty. "Absolute principles are intolerant of dissent," Dewey has pointed out, "for dissent from 'The Truth' is more than an intellectual error. It is proof of an evil and dangerous will." [43] If one side represents the good—wholly, unquestionably, and unconditionally—the other side must serve the Devil; and compromise with Satan is a sin, particularly in America, where the Devil is doubly damned as a foreign power. In democratic politics, compromise must be seen as more than an avenue that leads to the good; politically speaking, it is the good itself. A scientific measurement of a magnitude, say a length, is spoken of as an approximation to the "true length," but this "true length" is an abstraction constructed from an unending sequence of such measurements, or it has no meaning at all in experience. The good in a democracy must be operationally defined by democratic procedures. Granted that the working of these procedures is unsure, conditional, and approximative, and that their results are almost surely wrong in some respects and perhaps even altogether. Nevertheless, a free man must be free to go where he wills, even to perdition, if it lie on a road of his own choosing.

Americans recognize the usefulness of compromise in matters of expediency, but cannot countenance it in matters of morality.[44] What is a prudent concession in the one case becomes a cowardly appeasement in the other. If moral compromise be given a place in politics, what becomes of the crusade? And every political movement must be moralized as a crusade to enlist the support of right-thinking people. The work of the politician, however, is nothing but compromise; this is what it means to say that politics is the art of the practical. Practicality without compromise defines dictatorship. What the absolute moralist calls "dirty politics" is its natural condition; the adjective is redundant. The contempt in which the American politician is so often held today is not a mark of the deterioration of American statesmanship. Politicians have always been held in contempt. This is their business, as it is one of the functions of the psychiatrist to serve as a target for displaced hostility. The politician is the scapegoat for what an absolute morality regards as the sin of compromise. But when a necessity of nature becomes sinful, it is the morality that is unnatural.

In the end, an absolutistic moral code lowers the level of political morality, just as scientism weakens the genuine scientific impulse. It is not just that the standards absolutism imposes are impossible ones. The point is rather that in focusing on these standards in opposition to "relativism," it deflects attention and energy from the approximate values which political action can and must secure. The best is the worst enemy of the better, as Dewey has it. In human affairs, and certainly in democratic politics, more or less is the most that can be asked for. "Never hope to realise Plato's Republic. Let it be sufficient that you have in some slight degree ameliorated mankind, and do not think that amelioration a matter of small importance." This is the sentiment of Marcus Aurelius, himself a philosopher-king. It is a moral sentiment. And for all its air of Stoic resignation, it is a sentiment on which courageous men can act with determination on behalf of their political ideals.

MORALIZATION

American morality has a strong legalistic cast. Public morals are thought to be satisfied by conformity to public law, though the grounding of this law in "nature" allows morality to transcend purely political arrangements. But such arrangements are widely regarded as the proper instrument to secure moral values. Confronted with injustice, indecency, or iniquity of any kind, the American reaction is likely to be: "There oughta be a law!" The mere existence of the law is thought to suffice: the commandment—prohibition or a peace pact—magically brings about its own fulfillment. More accurately, it is a moralistic aspiration which is fulfilled. The enactment of the law, like a New Year's resolution, puts us on record on the side of morality, and thereby allays anxiety and guilt concerning our immoral impulses. It has been estimated that some ninety per cent of the population would be in jails if all our statutes were enforced. It is difficult even to imagine the enforcement of some of them—for instance, those regulating details of conjugal intimacies. Such statutes are empty, legally and—what is more to the point—morally. This hollow shell of morality is *moralization*.

The shell is largely verbalistic in character. In these matters Americans put great emphasis on the word, especially the written word. American constitutionalism, for example, contrasts markedly with the British, possibly because the younger and more heterogeneous society cannot rely so well on long-established custom. Whatever the reasons, in America concrete practices turn to abstract symbolisms for their justification. Legal issues are argued and decided by "the law" and "the courts," not by lawyers and judges. Conformity, whether social or moral, is sustained by appeal to "public opinion," "good citizenship," "civic responsibility." And in politics, the label is crucial—from "the New Deal" to "Modern Republicanism." There is no question here of cynical propaganda, like the use of the term "socialism" by European fascist parties. Americans believe what they say: in its own perspectives the Liberty League of Roosevelt's day was defending liberties, not privileges. His "economic royalists" were convinced democrats, that is to say, republicans—I mean equalitarians. And on the other side, the real constraints imposed by the state to maximize the range of real choices were verbalized as involving no loss of liberty at all. "The thousand dollar fur coat," Blondie explains, "was on sale for five hundred; but I saved five hundred, so it really cost me nothing!"

Philosophy has endorsed and even participated in such logic. An important part in American life is played by the grand occasions on which philosophers are called upon to make cosmic pronouncements. Few Americans would venture to deny that their politics and ethics, their whole scheme of values, rest upon what is called a "metaphysical basis." And to be really profound, it seems that such a metaphysics must be largely unintelligible. When Martin Buber accepted an appointment to the Hebrew University, he faced the task of learning to lecture in Hebrew; to a friend who some time afterward inquired about his progress in the language he replied, "I know enough now to make myself understood, but alas, not enough not to be understood!" Party platforms, preambles to constitutions, charters and declarations, solemn editorials—all play roles akin to that of the invocations of the Congressional chaplain. They have no bearing on the decisions to be made; but Americans would be uneasy at their absence.

In a word, moralization is the ritualistic use of the symbols of morality. Verbalizations are abstracted from their contextual references and felt to have a life of their own. The words go their own way and, far from being instruments of moral effort, can themselves bend moral aspirations to their own ends. The basic values of our public policy are thought to be embodied in "the American dream," "the American way of life," or simply "Americanism." But to our ears "the French dream" sounds obscene, "the German way of life" rigidly inhuman, and "Britishism" connotes snobbery and priggishness. Yet the interpretation is as projective in the first case as in the others. In the concrete, "the American way" is the way of Americans and nothing else; what way we are to choose as we face particular decisions is in no way defined by appeal to the ritualistic symbol. Anthropologists have long been aware that rituals precede the dogmas which rationalize them and also survive changes in these dogmas. But the wisdom of moral choice is independent of ritual and dogma alike.

What is at work here is the belief in verbal magic, in the power of the word itself to bring about a desired result. The magic, of course, lies in the mechanism of efficacy; there is no magic in achieving an open door by asking someone to open it. The magic lies in the open sesame which suffices of itself. The word imprisons the essence of the thing, which is released to do its work when the word is uttered; we are masters of the demon if we can speak his secret name. These are the fairy tales that we act out in politics when we rely on "free information" and the power of "the truth" for world-wide accord with our policies. This is the magic of securing loyalty by oaths, good citizenship by singing the national anthem at ball games, and patriotism by repainting our mail boxes in the colors of Old Glory. It is the superstition of the gentleman's agreement to a conspiracy of silence, lest the mention of discrimination give it an actuality it otherwise would not have. Nothing is fully real, we suppose, until it is verbalized. The facts of life need not be faced if we can find euphemisms by which they can be magically transformed.

The danger of these fantasies lies not in ritualism itself but in our taking the word for the deed, in ascribing to ritual an effectiveness in action which it does not have. In America, Laski points out, "there is an excessive love of the rhetoric of rights and a too easy belief that their declaration is their fulfillment." [45] Ringing pronouncements are mistaken for moral courage, the verbalization of ideals for moral achievement. It is in this perspective that Americans put so much reliance on promises as political instruments. The campaign promise is recognized in our own country for the ritual that it is, but in foreign affairs we distress other nations by habitually promising more than we intend to deliver, more even than we could deliver if we wanted to. In our own childishness we treat other nations like unruly children to be quieted with assurances of future delights.

All this is by no means exclusively American. In no other age have language and symbolism been so central to important developments in science, art, philosophy, and politics. Austrian psychoanalysis, French poetry, British philosophy, and nationalist politics everywhere have in the present century all turned on the uses and misuses of words and symbols. Other nations have relied much more than we on the clichés and stereotypes, the equivocations and empty abstractions of totalitarian Newspeak. Nevertheless, in America the formation of public policy, not just its public presentation, has been deeply infected with the virus of verbalism. We are recurrently tempted to formulate the problem of "understanding" the Russians as a disturbance of "communication," just as we suppose our national security to be threatened by subversive writings and defended by scientific "secrets."

In part, this cast of mind may be traceable to the fantastic growth of our mass media, all out of proportion to the development of our critical skills and our education in habits of reflection; to the unceasing impact of advertising on our lives; to the need for symbols by which to unify our heterogeneous subcultures, with no time for the slow growth of an organic unity; and to the immensity of the challenge to our survival, which stimulates search for a sign in which we can conquer. But perhaps most of all, our verbalism is an expression of what we call our youthful vigor and what others identify as our emotional immaturity. It is the infant to whom language is a most magically wondrous thing; the infantile adult finds it hard to realize that what he reads into his morality is words, words, words.

My objection to moralization is not simply the disparity between words and deeds. The semanticist fad which attacks all abstractions as unreal and all ideals as fictions betrays a fundamental misunderstanding of both science and morals. The function of ideals depends on their divergence from fact, as that of abstractions depends on their transcending the irrelevancies of concreta. An ideal is a direction of action, an order along a dimension; it is a moral objective as guiding action, not as specifying a point to be reached. The unattainability of ideals is a tautology, not a tribulation of the human condition. What is objectionable in a verbalistic morality is that its symbols function not as ideals but as utopias. They are points at infinity, unspecified both as to distance and direction. They do not guide moral action, but substitute for it.

It is a blunder to take the symbol for the fact that it symbolizes. But it is equally a blunder to fail to recognize the factuality of the symbol itself. Meaning is not another dimension perpendicular to reality, but adds a degree of freedom to our movement on the plane of reality. The recognition of the symbol as a fact of political life is perhaps the major contribution of twentieth-century political science—from the work of such European sociologists as Pareto and Mannheim, through the Chicago school of Merriam and Lasswell, to the countless contemporary studies of propaganda, public opinion, and political behavior. The belief in the effectiveness of symbols is not magical when these effects are

mediated by human responses to the symbols. The self-fulfilling predic-
tion of the propagandist is beginning to be understood in terms of the
mechanisms of social psychology; and Lasswell and others have illumi-
nated many facets of political life by conceiving them as resulting from
the displacement of private affects onto public objects—for instance,
through the symbols of family life so common in politics.[46]

Ritual as a cultural fact is to be neither dismissed nor deprecated.
It serves to intensify emotions and to make vivid meanings and values
grounded in the life of the culture. It is objectionable only when its
significance shrinks to its own performance, when it no longer draws
nourishment from realities outside the symbols. Such realities are the
sole source of the vitality of ritual; cut off from action it becomes a dry
husk, the letter that killeth. What ritualism is to the religious spirit,
moralization is to morality.

The words of the moralizer have no purchase on reality, and are not
intended to. This makes them objectionable, not their vagueness and
ambiguity, and certainly not their emotive force or appeal to the imagination. The moralist's conception of propaganda, within the framework
of the dualistic code, is to drop on the satellite populations either the
Sears catalog or the Bible, presumably according to the day of the week.
The trouble with the Russian leaders, we say, is that they are godless
men; if only they could be brought to read the Sermon on the Mount
and share our conviction that the meek shall inherit the earth! But until
then—what? Moralization, in cutting off morality from the springs of
action, leaves action without moral guidance. It has often been argued
against political verbalizations that historically they have been used in
defense of reaction, while the semantic critique has been a weapon of
reform. Maybe so. But the real danger here to morality is not that
verbalizations will be invoked in support of the wrong policies. It is that
verbalistic moralizing will interfere with deciding which policy is the
wrong one.

In moralistic perspectives, not policy but people are judged. The
moralist views politics as a drama of good and evil. His interest focuses
on character. The moralistic analysis is directed to persons, not institutions, and to policies only as expressions of personality, not as the out-
comes of institutional constraints. Whatever happens is ascribed to
human agency, benevolent or malicious. The task of politics is only

to throw the rascals out; with the right men in office there is nothing to worry about. People are good or bad and *therefore* policies are; the measure of the policy is the moral stature of the policy maker. Thus politics is personalized, personality moralized.[47] Governments are reacted to in terms of their representatives, and these, in turn, on the basis of the moral categories we project onto them. If our allies take important steps without consulting us, we respond with a sense of personal injury, not with a reappraisal of the policies that forfeited their trust and confidence. The moralizer, in short, formulates moral issues in terms of character and motive, not action and consequences. That is why verbalization is so congenial to him: it allows morality to be abstracted from action, internalized, and refined—until it becomes an altogether ghostly thing.

I do not mean to deny the importance of character in both politics and morals. On the contrary, I have already identified character as the element of unity in moral action, the integrity of political decision. But the moralizer misconceives character as an agglomeration of moralistic virtues, and he allows these to replace the wisdom of the moral agent and the judgment of the political leader. He looks for religiosity, patriotism, and simplicity; and if to these homey virtues there is added a driving sense of duty, the moralizer in politics asks for nothing more. His ideal among American statesmen is not Lincoln but William Jennings Bryan.

On the contemporary political scene, such stature as Bryan had has shrunk altogether to the level of boyish charm; moral indignation has given way to sentimentality, the old-time evangelist to the moral salesman for a mass market. The passion for ideals and principles which animates the moralizer is hard to distinguish, in its most distinguished representatives, from soap opera emotionalism. Moral sentiment, however, is not necessary to even the most elevated morality, as Buddha, Socrates and Spinoza attest, by what they were as well as by what they taught. And it is not sufficient either: the maudlin Christmas card and Christmas carol do not make a Christian life. But sentiment is easy to express, easy to recognize, easy to share; and, in a democracy, the pure of heart whom the moralizer calls for must wear his heart on his sleeve. The patriot must broadcast his patriotism on a national hookup. Liza

Doolittle might have become a congresswoman with her repeated declaration, "I'm a lady, I am!"

This is to say that moralization provides only a projected image of the moral life, as glamour objectifies only the fantasy of love. The bifurcation of appearance and reality thus reappears in the metaphysics of morals, as an expression of an ambivalence within the moral self, an inner conflict between private practice and public standards, between what we do and the shared pretense of what we are. The advertiser sexualizes every commodity (except breakfast cereals), but no one must notice it; just as the movie queen must look seductive while preserving the image of underlying chastity. We glorify the home whatever the rate of delinquency and divorce, and sentimentalize childhood while refusing to rent to couples with "children or pets." We condemn gambling and quote the odds, abjure state lotteries and take our cut at the track. As I have said elsewhere, conventional moralization is tyranny tempered by hypocrisy. And it is hard to say whether we are more hypocritical in our virtue or in our vice.

In the light of the great political problems of our time all this is trivial, but just this is the important point. Moralization trivializes morality, reducing virtue to a denial of the senses and moral principles to the prohibitions of a backwoods boardinghouse. Bryce reports that in America ". . . the average of temperance, chastity, truthfulness, and general probity is higher than in any of the great nations of Europe." This is probably still true; but a simple-minded eunuch with stomach ulcers would also be a paragon of these virtues. There is great moralizing zeal in America, Bryce continues, but it is directed to the same trivial ends: ". . . to suppress vice, to prevent intemperance, to purify popular literature." [48] Such morality, as I stated earlier, is felt to be feminine or childishly submissive. Its virtues are those of the "good little boy." The moralizer can neither wholly reject them, for they are virtues, nor wholly accept them, for he is a man. So he preserves self-respect by isolating virtue from effective action.

Where in this trivialized morality can we find the prophetic grandeur of social ethics? Moralism thinks to emulate Lincoln with passion toward none and philanthropy for all. Its code is essentially the control of libido, but not of aggression. Yet if we are to speak—as the moralist continually does—of the decay of morality in the present age, surely "free love" wears an incomparably less hideous aspect than "free hate." The American novelist and screenwriter may portray in detail a man killing a woman, but not one making love to her. To be sure, the pornography of violence is also condemned: the moralist has taken up arms against it, he will fight it to the death, he will destroy it utterly. And thus the hatred of evil can become an acceptable excuse—for hate. This is not to say flatly that aggression in all forms is wicked, as gentler versions of moralism have it. The moral problem is to externalize aggression and direct it against its proper objects. That is the moral problem with libido as well. The moralist feeds his prurience in his search for purity, and tries to master his own impulses by censoring the impulses of others. "Thou shalt not love, thou shalt not hate"—no wonder the moralist is felt to be lacking in simple humanity!

It is not Puritanism which is here in question. As a religious tradition, Puritanism is perhaps less influential in America than are the various evangelical, revivalist denominations. Just as Plato's Eros was scarcely platonic but in fact the creative principle, what is often called "puritanical" is not an austere self-denial but a single-minded devotion to self-advancement. In this ethic, sensory gratification is condemned, not because it is an indulgence, but because it interferes with work—its price is exorbitant, its pleasure is transient. But if it can refresh the tired businessman, it has its place. What is preached is Theodore Roosevelt's doctrine of "the strenuous life"; even William James defined moral action as "action in the line of greatest resistance." [49] These are the perspectives invited by an expanding frontier and an equalitarian society that provides an unlimited opportunity for advancement of the self through mastery of the environment. Such perspectives are much less important today, though something of Prometheus and Faust has been an enduring and admirable strain in the American character. But that strain, absolutized and moralized, degenerates to the fault Shaw (in *Man and Superman*) so incisively laid to the British—"Your pious English habit of regarding the world as a moral gymnasium built expressly to strengthen your character in, occasionally leads you to think about your own confounded principles when you should be thinking about other people's necessities." What the Devil later in the play remarks about the Englishman applies to the American moralist as well: he "thinks he is moral when he is only uncomfortable."

The political impact of these perspectives is considerable. American politics has often been characterized as combining both religion and sport. But in recent years much of the sportsmanship has disappeared; what remains is the ritual and a highly charged moralistic rhetoric. Self-righteousness has been carried to such a point that the opposition party is almost made to feel immoral for carrying on a campaign at all. Other countries are understandably dismayed by our offensive pose of unswerving rectitude. "A nation forgives if its interests have been damaged," Weber wrote some decades ago, "but no nation forgives if its honor has been offended, especially by a bigoted self-righteousness." [50]

Worst of all, this attitude leads to the preposterous analysis of political problems as turning solely on ethical considerations. How many times have we been told that "the crisis of the times is moral, and the only hope for democracy depends upon whether it can revitalize itself as a moral force"! [51] We have been using enough and more than enough of this "moral force" in Hungary and the Middle East; I am not aware that it was "moral force" that carried the day in Korea. Yet the cry endlessly goes up for "spiritual regeneration." When the diagnosis is unvarying—a moral failing—moralization becomes the irresistible prescription. [52]

Yet moralization is not without a genuine moral quality—far be it from me to deny that there is any good in men of virtue! Though the moralist does not recognize the Devil in his most effective guises, still he fights the powers of hell wherever he encounters them. He may be lacking in moral insight, but he does have a species of moral courage. There is no quietism in the moralistic outlook, no passive resignation to the evil that men do. Wherever something calls for betterment, the moralist stands ready to answer the call. His efforts may be misdirected to amelioration of immediate consequences rather than to removal of underlying causes—as in his vast philanthropies—but they are moral efforts nevertheless. The continuing myth that Americans worship the dollar is a European—and now also Asiatic—defense mechanism against the actualities of American generosity. The moralist may be right after all: it is more blessed to give than to receive.

Most truly moral is American sympathy for the underdog, the underprivileged, the man who has been left out. European observers have always been struck by our kindly good nature; what is really striking is that they find it so noteworthy. "Nowhere," Bryce says, "is cruelty more abhorred. Even a mob lynching a horse thief in the West has consideration for the criminal and will give him a good drink of whiskey before he is strung up." [53]

It is even possible that Bryce was in dead earnest. Americans, at any rate, are in earnest about their kindliness. Though our policy of being a "good neighbor" is a typically moralistic formulation, it verbalizes for politics a real constituent of our personal lives. "If it were given me to look into the depths of a man's heart, and I did not find goodwill at the bottom, I should say without any hesitation, You are not an American." [54] No American, I think, will quarrel with this opinion of Santayana's; no one who knows Americans will lightly dismiss it. But the question is still to be asked whether goodwill alone can bring peace on earth.

THE CODE OF CONFORMITY

For all the talk of modernism, scepticism, and the collapse of moral authority, the working morality of America is largely traditional. Of course, there have been changes in customs and manners, as well as persisting differences among our many subcultures. The importance of such changes and differences is often underestimated; some kinds of diversity continue to be welcomed. But by and large, the American moral code follows traditional lines.

To say that it is traditional is not to say that it is mistaken. I am bringing into question not the content of the morality, but its basis— its warrant, not its worth. Morals everywhere are the outgrowth of mores: the right way of doing things is the way they have "always" been done. But from its beginnings America has prided itself on a willingness to subject tradition to rational scrutiny. In one of the *Federalist Papers* Madison asks, "Is it not the glory of the people of America that, whilst they have paid a decent regard to the opinions of former times and other nations, they have not suffered a blind veneration for antiquity, for custom, or for names, to overrule the suggestions of their own good sense, the knowledge of their own situation, and the lessons of their own experience?" [55] It can scarcely be denied that something of this glory has faded. Veneration for antiquity, custom, and names makes up a considerable part of the impassioned and sometimes hysterical defense of "the American way of life."

Our adherence to the authority of tradition is not overt and self-conscious. On the contrary, in both religion and politics the tradition itself is explicitly anti-authoritarian. Individual conscience and personal experience are called upon for support of policy, moral intuition rather than received dogmas of Church and State. But moral intuition has a social history; when it becomes absolute and moralistic it provides an internalized channel by which the authority of tradition can take effect. The right way is what conscience proclaims to be right; but conscience proclaims it because it is the way followed in the culture by which conscience itself was shaped.

The morality of conscience is thus still, in terms of the classic contrast, a customary rather than a reflective morality. Virtue is taken to be a matter of heart and soul, not sense and intellect. The eighteenth-century program of summoning tradition before the bar of reason has been replaced in the twentieth by a pervasive fear for traditional values felt to be threatened by the critical intelligence. The successful candidate is the man who appears safe, the conservative with the forward look. Only when traditional patterns collapse in crisis is there a disposition to turn to the man of boldness and imagination. As for the critical and reflective temper, it has little place in politics at all.

What makes a morality a matter of custom is more than respect for tradition. Not only the past but also the present fixes its content. In both cases the content derives from a source external to the moral agent. His way of life is determined by submission to a standard set by others. What begins as "a decent respect for the opinions of mankind" ends in a thoroughgoing "other-directedness." Thereby morality is brought back to its starting point in the mores. It becomes a matter of good form, good taste, respect for the conventions—in a word, conformity. An immoral act is simply something which is "not done," righteousness reduces to propriety, and the good is nothing other than the established order of things. The sense of wrongdoing is marked by shame rather than by guilt. And there is no need for a man to decide whether he would rather be right than president; the majority that elects the president thereby determines what is right. If only you conform to the majority, he is right and you are right and all is right as right can be.

But is Emerson no longer to be counted an American? "Whoso would be a man must be a nonconformist!" Oh yes, Emerson is quoted often enough; quoting Emerson—and Jefferson and Lincoln—is itself a propriety, one to which I have already paid my respects and will again! But the slogans of nonconformism usually function in fact only to strengthen the patterns of conformity. We are all alike in priding ourselves on being different; we enforce uniformity in the pretense of inviting deviation. When Russell was jailed as a pacifist in the First World War he identified his religion as "Atheist," to which the bailiff replied, "Ah well, I suppose we all worship the same God whatever we call Him!" Conformism reaches its limit when noncomformist patterns are beyond understanding.

American love of diversity is a traditional verbalization (and perhaps the same is true of my own criticism of conformity!). Orators and editors speak at length about the harmonious orchestration of our many cultural themes, about the beauty of the American mosaic fashioned from bits and pieces of such divergent cultural origins. But our practice often accords with the more traditional metaphor of the melting pot, which is boiling more furiously today than during the years of heavy immigration. In recent polls, two-thirds of the population would not allow anyone to make a speech in the community against churches and religion; only one in eight would allow such a person to teach.[56] Russell was thought to be unfit to hold a position at the City College of New York; and when Laski was in this country a few years ago, a great university found reason to cancel his scheduled lecture.

These are isolated cases, to be sure, and of foreigners besides; but no purpose would be served here by statistical documentation. Regardless of ritualistic reassurances, we are not in competition for an Olympic award as the freest nation on earth. Will we never judge ourselves by standards of our own making? In willing unity as an end we have bound ourselves to conformist pressures as means, and these, in turn, can grow into the regimentation we detest as tyranny. The zone of privacy has been steadily shrinking before the inroads of the police, the press, the advertiser, the employer, and officious persons everywhere. Let us by all means congratulate ourselves that Big Brother is not yet watching; but we must also commiserate with each other for prying cousins.

In the name of "Americanism" the right to private opinion is most often sacrificed. What a man reads, with whom he associates, how he understands foreign affairs—these are not his own concern, in the perspective of the Americanists, but must be brought into public view and scrutinized for any possible threat to the security of our way of life. "To be an American is of itself almost a moral condition, an education, and a career." Santayana wrote these words over thirty years ago.[57] In the last decade several careers—of men without either morals or education—have consisted of little else. For a time the forum of public discussion was closed to any arguments but those leading to foregone conclusions. Everything else was proscribed as "controversial"—to defend a system of government by controversy, for democracy is just that. We remain free of the despotism of censorship; but pre-censorship—the fear of subsequent reaction—operates strongly still, especially in the mass media. Our laws guarantee freedoms which are weakened by informal pressures before ever the courts can be invoked in their defense. We are still to achieve a "moral emancipation" which as yet "is but nominal with us. The inquisition of public opinion overwhelms in practice the freedom asserted by the laws in theory." The American whose help I am calling on is—need I say it?—Thomas Jefferson. There are few who would claim that since his day the inquisition of public opinion has lessened in intensity.

The Americanist proceeds by personalizing the basis of political debate. What is brought into question is not only the opponent's program and policies, but also his motives and character. Issues come to be formulated solely in terms of the comparative loyalty of the conflicting parties. Political ideas are appraised only according to whether they are safe or dangerous. I do not mean to deny that loyalties have been betrayed in the Communist conspiracy, that security faces risks, or even that ideas can be dangerous. The danger of ideas, as of every other instrument, is inseparable from their efficacy. The same force that makes any instrumentality a power for good can also work corresponding evil. The Americanist's conclusion follows logically from his premise; if we are to be secure from this danger, we must either proscribe ideas altogether or remove them from the plane of action. Democracy, in my understanding, rejects the premise; it is committed to living dangerously, compelling assent only by the force of ideas. To achieve greatly we must dare greatly. Above all, we must dare to live with heresy and even, as our individual judgments dictate, to be occasional heretics ourselves.

If only God Himself identified the orthodox! But in a democracy there is no agency external to the democratic process to serve as absolute judge of right and wrong. Orthodoxy is simply the view supported at a given historical moment by the preponderant force of the community. To fix Americanism forever in that moment is to deny its past and destroy its future. Life is defined once for all only in death; a way of life is as variable and plastic as the people who live it. It may be frozen in ideology, but even that demands interpretation, an act *within* history, for each day as that day declares it. Orthodoxy and heresy may change places—and revert again—as values find actuality or lose it in the specific choices of concrete action. The Americanism of the Americanists is as bleak and immobile as the shadows etched in concrete at Hiroshima.

The code of conformity, in binding the future to the past, betrays its lack of a sense of history. In offering itself as the sole standard of right and wrong, it reveals its blindness to the present as well. Differences in American values can as easily be found by moving from one person to another as from one time to another. We each define the good in our own perspectives, as our own experience dictates. "Every man, for his own part, calls that which pleases and is delightful to himself, *good*; and that *evil* which displeases him; in so much that while every man differs from another in constitution, they differ also one from another concerning the common distinction of good and evil." This analysis of the moral judgment is in the words of Hobbes; it is fundamental in Spinoza's ethics, and has been reaffirmed by almost every naturalistic philosopher since. Shaw's Revolutionist drew from it the moral that we should *not* do unto others as we would have them do unto us: their tastes may differ. We must either respect these differences or else forgo democracy to impose a code from above. We will not protest if the imposed values be to *our* taste; but how if *their* tastes govern?

The code of conformity takes for granted the superiority of the orthodox values. The question is, however, not which is "really" better, but what meaning can attach to a comparison at all? To speak of "better" is to presuppose someone *for* whom it is better—not the person in whose judgment it is such, but the person whose experience of good is being judged. It is the relativity of value I am urging, not its subjectivity. Comparisons of value are odious when they overlook the essence of the values compared: the needs, interests, and tastes whose satisfaction is the very ground of value. Objective differences in these make for objective differences in value, however great the conformist pressures forcing valuations into a single mold. In our Father's house are many mansions; the plurality of values does not undermine the worth of any. The bogey of relativism is frightening only when we mistake it for subjectivism—as though the dependence of value on differing human desires makes the satisfaction of desire a matter of mere think-so. The varieties of human value are just beginning to be empirically explored; in the perspectives of conformism, such an exploration will produce only a catalog of human folly and perversity. Fortunately, only a minority of Americans have yielded this much to conformist pressures.

Critics of American culture have been given to loose talk about the evils of "standardization" and have made of difference itself an absolute good. There has been much foolish romanticism in connection with defiance of convention and self-conscious "originality." American technology, however, has demonstrated to all the world the human worth of standardized means, interchangeable parts, instrumentalities designed for application under the widest range of conditions. The resultant increase in the productivity of labor contributes significantly to the good life however that be conceived. The criticism has been superficial because it directed itself against standardization as such; and it has been futile because the value of standardization is now a commonplace of universal experience. What is objectionable is the unthinking extension of these technological perspectives to ends as well as means, to the values sought as well as to the ways pursued in the seeking. We have succeeded brilliantly in providing the one right tool for every job; but we have too often supposed that there is only one job for every right-thinking man, only one way of life, only one set of values.

Differences here are felt to be even more distressing than in the gauges of adjoining railroads. "We must . . . dissolve particularism," the conformist tells us, "vary the mixture indefinitely, disseminate all traits, enrich ourselves by permutation and combination. Anything else is the vicious circle of neurotic irritation and neurotic fear." [58] It is in this attitude itself that I find the irritation and fear. Differences in value engender conflict only in the perspectives of a conformism irritated by difference, not in the view of an accepting pluralism. We are impelled to destroy differences only when we are fearful of our capacities to live with them. In truth, the life of a democracy is a continuing conflict of values and its continuing resolution. The conformist is intolerant of difference because he has no tolerance within himself for the give and take of democratic decision making. If he can be sure of agreement beforehand, there will be no decisions to make. Failing this, he can at least look to a happy future when all differences will have disappeared in a realm of value rich and creamy with homogenized goodness.

It is always possible to make it appear that values are uniform, by concealing real differences behind a verbal sameness. Is not the emancipation of man from bondage to other men a communistic as well as a democratic ideal, social justice the aim of both patterns of social organization? In the abstract, yes; but the concrete meanings given to these ideals by specific practices and institutions are very different. If freedom of the press, for instance, is conceived as the right of the people to know the truth, and truth is held to be definable only by governmental authority, a state-controlled press will be thought to be free. We are ourselves the victims of this Soviet semantics if we identify values only because they bear the same names (or distinguish them only because they are differently labeled). Everyone, surely, seeks "justice," or at any rate recognizes that he ought to do so. But this is to say only that the desirability of the thing is part of the meaning of the word; what does not answer to our aspirations we do not recognize as being "really just." Similarly, we can produce a show of unity by focusing on "ultimate" ends, sufficiently remote for crucial differences in proximate policy to vanish in the distance. No doubt Israel and Egypt both want a resolution of the crisis in the Middle East. But it would be naive to suppose that this ultimate end of enduring peace represents the basis for agreement; on the contrary, the concrete meaning of "peace" for each of them is precisely what divides them. Two chess players both wanting a draw can quickly agree on the outcome of the game; but to say that they both want a checkmate is to point precisely to what makes them antagonists.

The logic of such situations is absurdly simple; alas, policy formation sometimes seems to follow a peculiar logic of its own, particularly when moral considerations come into play. I propose to call this blindness to real differences in value because of abstract and verbalistic sameness the *eudaemonian* fallacy, from Aristotle's term for happiness as the universally acknowledged good. Nietzsche's aphorism that man does not desire happiness, but only the Englishman does, is more than a jibe at bourgeois values. It directs attention to a narrower sense of the term in which it designates values that are far from universal. This duality of meaning is basic to the structure of the fallacy; in its broader sense the fallacious generalization is true but empty, and in its narrower sense significant but false. This equivocation has been pointed out many times with respect to the view that all men are fundamentally selfish. This confuses the truism that the satisfaction of each of my desires satisfies me, with the falsehood that what I desire is only my own satisfaction. The alleged universality of the profit motive is another case in point. In the broad sense of "profit" as any accession of good, it is tautologous that all action is undertaken for profit. In its specifically economic sense, this is patently false, even with regard to action in the economic sphere. Work is motivated also by what Veblen called "the instinct of workmanship," by ideals of service, by a desire for self-respect or the respect of others, by devotion to the good of the organization or even to the greater glory of God. In short, the *eudaemonian* fallacy finds a single-ness of purpose behind the multiplicity of concrete values only by artificially abstracting values from the context of action which alone gives them meaning.

By such an abstraction the conformist can assure himself that American values are universal, that underneath it all other peoples prize just what we do. Such differences as he recognizes he ascribes to ignorance, to the lack of natural endowments—especially of character—and, most of all, to the pernicious influence of wicked leaders. Of course he can tolerate minor differences in political forms, as in the British monarchy or French parliamentarianism—though unquestionably the American political system is the best. But the basic values to which he demands domestic conformity he also expects to dominate the international scene. The American Way is intended for export, and for the best of reasons: America has, in Theodore Roosevelt's words, "a responsibility for the moral welfare of others which cannot be evaded." [59] Notice: not a moral responsibility for their welfare as *they* conceive it, but a responsibility for their *moral* welfare as *we* conceive it. America is the custodian of world morality, on behalf of history, posterity, or God. If we cannot see to the establishment of American values everywhere, we must at least secure their existence here. There is continuing pressure on our foreign policy—though it has progressively lessened in recent decades—to address itself only to this limited objective and let the rest of the world go hang. But if we are to concern ourselves with the welfare of others, there can be no real question what their welfare consists in: it is to be as much like Americans as they can possibly manage.

This is the posture in which for decades Europe and Asia have stereotyped the American: a moralistic imperialist imposing on others his puritanism and vulgarity to cover his sordid material interests. It is understandable that other nations should regard as insufferable conceit the presumption that only the American way of life embodies the true faith, while everything else is sin and superstition. The irony is that what the posture really expresses is a deep-seated insecurity. Our missionary zeal is rooted in a hope for our own conversion. When conformity serves as the standard of value, the mere existence of other values brings our own into question. Therefore there must be no others. The conformist wants nothing so much as to be accepted, to be liked. Popularity marks him as one of the Lord's anointed; it is at once the sign and the substance of his Election. This is what motivates the tendency to universalize American values; it is a wish-fulfilling fantasy to allay the anxieties of being left alone with values whose worth depends on others.

Accordingly, American foreign relations are conducted in the perspectives of salesmanship: we must "sell" our policies to other nations, and we can do so only by selling ourselves. The superiority of American values thus becomes a primary theme of American diplomacy as well as one of its working presuppositions. But we cannot quite believe in this superiority ourselves unless it is first acknowledged by others. The important thing, then, is to make ourselves liked, and it is to this end that we direct our efforts. It does not occur to us, however, to formulate policies that are also in the interest of those we want as allies. Instead we undertake to buy friendship, then rightly distrust the love that is for sale. We are forever looking for the prostitute with the heart of gold.

Conformism itself lays bare the dynamics of this insecurity. In the last century, the great mobility of American society made it hard for a man to know what his place was, what was rightfully his, and what was expected of him. In the present century, the narrowing of opportunity has made it doubly unsure where a man can get to, and whether he can remain at whatever height he reaches. Intensified competition engenders hostility, evokes fear both of failure and of reprisals for competitive success, and leads finally to the insecurities of emotional isolation. This line of analysis goes back at least to Spinoza: a man's security can rest only on what he is in his own nature. To measure ones' worth by a comparative standing, by conformity to norms externally imposed, is precisely what constitutes human bondage.

The final cost of the code of conformity is the sacrifice of leadership. The role of the leader it assigns to the most successful follower, the man whose features can best reflect at every moment the changing face of the crowd. Bryce was surely prescient when he wrote, "In America the practical statesman is apt to be timid in advocacy as well as infertile in suggestion. He seems to be always listening for the popular voice, always afraid to commit himself to a view which may turn out unpopular." [60] We have had some very "practical" statesmen, and television and the polls make them more "practical" every day. Leadership requires the maintenance of a certain distance from the followers, enough to give scope for independent judgment and decisive action. But this in turn calls for courage and self-confidence, not the sheepish virtues of conformity to a preformed opinion. Such a man may not always be liked; he may even expect to make some enemies. But to be able to lead others a man must be willing to go forward alone.

MORALITY AND POWER

In many ways the American moral code is absolutistic and conformist. Yet a great gulf divides it from the absolutism of the dictatorships, the regimented conformity of the totalitarian states. The key to this difference lies in the relationship of morality to power. In America the force of the state does not define morality but is itself continually subjected to the moral judgment of the citizen. Granted that in many areas of action American legalism tries to reduce morality to law; in business and politics whatever is within the law is conventionally acceptable. But this holds true largely for such peripheral matters as a corporation's payment of taxes or a legislator's acceptance of gifts. A critical business policy or political decision may at any time raise moral issues recognized as not settled—or, at any rate, as not yet settled—by the law. Our dualistic perspectives make for a tendency to polarize morality and power. In foreign affairs we are likely to rely on the affirmation of abstract moral principles together with the use of amoral economic pressures; a habit of thought which would concretize the principles and give moral significance to the pressures is foreign to us. Yet there remains a real sense of moral responsibility in political commitment. We may distrust as "propaganda" explicitly ideological formulations—even our own. But there is an unwavering insistence on the application of moral standards to political action. The will of the state is an expression of one kind of power; but morality lies in the power expressed as the will of the people.

Only the will of the people democratically justifies the action of the state. The power of the state rests on a moral basis; democracy agrees with Aristotle and Aquinas in viewing the state as an agency of moral order. This is the significance of the American tradition of natural rights; it is to secure these rights that governments are instituted among men. Once established, of course, governments define legal obligations to themselves. But these are morally binding only as the government, for its part, discharges its moral obligations. When government becomes destructive of moral ends, it is the right of the people to alter or abolish it. There is no autonomous political obligation distinct from moral obligation and its legal offspring. Democratic political theorists from Locke to Laski have insisted on this moralizing of power, in contrast to the totalitarian practice of politicizing even morality.

The historian of political ideas may rightly point out that Marx too had a moral objective. His materialism was metaphysical, not moral; there is no hedonism in it. It is a dangerous error to suppose that the appeal of communism—to the literate, at any rate—lies in its offer to fill the belly. The promise that Marx held out was rather to free the worker from wage slavery and to liberate the works of the human spirit from the status of mere commodities.[61] But there is also a danger here of succumbing to the eudaemonian fallacy. The question is not one of ultimate ends but of the proximate policies pursued in the name of these ends. Whatever its principles, in fact the communist elite treats the mass as something to be manipulated. The mass constitutes the means and the material by which the elite is to attain the ends of the state. Democratic ethics falls back on Kant rather than Hegel: in accord with Kant's categorical imperative, man is never to be treated as a means only, even if it be for the ends of history as Hegel conceived it. The concept of "exploitation" does not derive from the economics of surplus value; it is a moral category. Man is exploited when he is subjected to power without moral restraint.

The American moral code insists on limiting power by this restraint. Justice is not simply the interest of the stronger, the decision of the sovereign, or the policy of the ruling class. On this score American ethics has no use for Thrasymachus, Hobbes, or Lenin. The concept of "bourgeois morality" may make sense as designating the particular values of a particular social class, but not as identifying the ground of moral value with class interest, just as "class science" may point to what a class *believes* to be true without in the least undermining the objective basis of scientific truth. The reduction of morality to power pushes the basis of moral appraisal into a region wholly inaccessible to experience—the relation of the sovereign to God or of the proletarian dictator to history. Confronted with tyranny, Americans are not content with the assurance that history will provide its ultimate justification. Our attitude to the tyrant is not "Leave him to Heaven" but "Leave him to us!" The people must judge, and they must judge now.

It is not the political organization of the economic system that distinguishes the "People's Republics" from government of, by, and for the people. Democracy can accommodate whatever degree of economic planning or socialization emerges from the democratic process itself; some degree may even be necessary for the preservation of the process. The decisive question is whether the power applied in the economic sphere is subject to appraisal by the moral values underlying both politics and economics. What constitutes "statism" is not the range of welfare functions assumed by the state but the moral claim made by the state in performnig those functions. Similarly, a sense of history is as necessary to democratic statesmanship as it is to any other; but in a democracy, historical fact does not of itself define moral value. In these terms, the multiplicity of social philosophies can be brought into intelligible order without the crude simplifications of "freedom versus authority."

The theories of the organic state of English absolute idealism give primacy to the state as more metaphysically "real" than the empirical individuals that compose it. The locus of morality is thought to lie in this larger whole, the national community whose actions produce the movement of history. In fascism, the career of the state not only constitutes history but also defines the substance of morality, which is identified with the needs of the state at each historical juncture. Other social philosophies make history primary. For the social Darwinists, as for Nietzsche and Spengler, morality is defined by the historical process, the state being one expression among others of the spirit of the age. Hegel and Marx view history as working through the state; morality is meaningful only in relation to the dialectic of reason or the forces of production which provide the dynamics of history. Finally, morality may be put in first place. Judaeo-Christian thought conceives of history as embodying a universal moral order instituted by Divine Providence; the state is an instrumentality of this order. Democracy shares this insistence on the primacy of the moral. But it interprets the state directly in terms of moral ideals, and not through a chiliastic philosophy of history. For democracy, history is forever in the making. The Fall and the Redemption are enacted anew in each moment of moral choice.

Every state brings power into some relation with morality. Naked power must somehow be clothed in the robes of authority so that coercion can be internalized. The stability of the state depends on a widespread sense of the legality of its power, by which obedience to law is grounded in something more than fear. Unless a revolution is, in Lasswell's phrase, a rupture of conscience, any shift in the balance of power in the state can provide the basis for a new structure of authority. The state, in short, requires a principle of legitimacy by which it can command the continuing loyalty of its subjects and not just their passing obedience.

The possession of power, together with the capacity to exercise it, can itself be made to serve as such a principle. The sword belongs to him who has the strength to draw it and the courage to wield it. Might makes right when the maintenance of order is given primacy among political values and the evils of anarchy are thought to outweigh any others. Machiavelli is only superficially amoral: the unification of Italy was for him the political ideal by which the power of the prince was legitimized. Similarly, fascist political thought must obviously be understood in terms of the social disorganization of Europe in the decades following the First World War. In America order is not an absolute value, and scarcely even a major political concern. Yet our ideals of efficiency and success lend themselves to a similar political application. Between the wars our vulgar pragmatists have had a grudging—and sometimes even wholehearted—admiration for Hitler and Mussolini.

The identification of de facto with de jure power is not wholly absurd. American moralism has sometimes thrust out of consciousness the facts of political life, so that empirically recognizable power is denied formal recognition far beyond the point where the formality is serviceable as an instrument of diplomacy. Recognition may be withheld on moralistic grounds, rather than on the basis of a realistic appraisal of the moral values that are politically possible in the situation. The enduring contribution to political thought of the Machiavellians—Mosca, Michels, and Pareto, as well as their eponym—is their insistence on the facts of power as basic to any realistic morality of power. What is morally objectionable in Realpolitik is not that these facts are made central in politics but that they are identified, as is, with political values. Power politics is politics that takes power as an end in itself and as the sole and absolute end of political action. The refusal to countenance power as having any moral standing at all is not the antithesis to power politics but its moralistic counterpart. Political idealism which renounces power altogether achieves only the empty virtue of the impotent.

There is another principle of legitimacy: the conception of the state as fulfilling a mission accepted as moral—and even as defining morality—by the subjects of the state. Such a principle secularizes the divine right of kings, replacing God by history and the workings of Providence by historical forces. The Marxist dialectic is a political Manicheism: the class struggle re-enacts on earth the cosmic conflict between God and Satan. Politics in this perspective becomes a calling, and the vanguard of the proletariat serves as a priesthood—dedicated and self-denying. In the light of this personal asceticism, the moralistic concern with "corruption" sadly misconceives the moral issues raised by the exercise of power.

In the politics of Destiny it is still the Judaeo-Christian drama of man's fate that is being enacted, but in a secular production. Hitler's

Teutonic mythology and the New Order, Mussolini's Caesarism, primitive communism and world socialism—all these have the moral significance of paradise lost and paradise regained. The drama differs from the religious version chiefly in its holism: its protagonist is not the individual soul but the race, nation, or class. In American political life historicism reveals itself in the appeal of policy to historical patterns for meaning and justification: a linear pattern in the progressive's perspectives of continuous improvement in an unending future; cyclical in the reactionary's longing for a golden past to which we must return; or shrunken to a fixed point in the present, in the conservative's defense of a closed social order. For liberal democracy, past, present, and future are all three implicated in public policy. Paradoxically, historicism denies the reality of time, making of it, as Plato did, a moving image of an eternity where the solution to all human problems is already prefigured.

It is tempting to formulate policy by reference to a cause which must ultimately triumph, and Americans of many political persuasions have yielded to the temptation. We have usually rejected not the politics of destiny but only the mission claimed by other nations. It is the secularism that has offended our moral sense, not the historicism. We have not always seen clearly that a historic mission, whatever its content, divorces power from morality.[62] Policy that is realistically concerned with human values cannot be formulated in terms of Causes, but only in terms of the real possibilities for good in concrete political situations. We cannot discharge our moral obligations once and for all simply by pledging allegiance to America's mission of morality. We cannot realistically hope to succeed in our moral aspirations unless our fantasies of predestined success give way to sober appraisals of the risk of failure.

For most Americans what legitimizes power is the doctrine of representation. A man has the right to do as he chooses for himself; that right is transferred to the state insofar as the state represents him. What this presupposes, as Locke and Rousseau saw, is that there is no fixed social order into which the citizen is born, for otherwise his choice would be limited from the outset in ways which representation could not justify. It presupposes also a code of representation, a standard of performance by which the constituency can judge whether their representative is indeed representing them. It is in this responsibility to the people that the moral restraint on power is localized. Power is legitimate when it governs by consent of the governed. The doctrine of natural rights does not go deep enough in its attempt to provide a moral foundation for power. For what the rights come to in experience requires interpretation; if power is to be justified by its efforts to secure these rights, their interpretation must rest with the people. Morality is inseparable from freedom; the moral use of power is inseparable from a free consent to its exercise.

American moralism, however, sentimentalizes "the people." It imagines that popular sovereignty and civil liberties will inevitably result in the right decision. And so they will—provided that the "rightness" of the decision is recognized to be procedural and not substantive. A belief arrived at on the basis of the available evidence is necessarily a rational belief, but it is not necessarily a true one. The democratic process of decision making is justified by the moral aim of developing free and mature personalities. It does not and cannot find justification by a pretense of unerring wisdom in the people. Plato's arguments for a philosopher-king are logically sound—how could I deny it! But they are entirely beside the point. There is no doubt that an elite might make better decisions; but the question is whether it is better even so that they do the deciding. The voice of the people is the voice of God; only, what the people speaks in that voice is its own mind.

The American insistence that popular support for a policy is necessary to its morality seems to me unexceptionable. But we believe too easily that the consent of the people is sufficient for morality. We suppose that the force of public opinion itself provides the moral restraint on power, and particularly do we think so with respect to what we call "world opinion." What this belief overlooks is that consent can be cajoled as well as coerced; virtue is lost to seduction more often than to rape. Hitler was elected by a democratic majority under the Weimar Constitution; Communist candidates would win even free elections behind the Iron Curtain as long as the voters themselves are not free. Spinoza's rationalism is as important for democratic theory as Locke's empiricism.

The moralistic doctrine is that "the people" everywhere are good, kind, wise, and friendly. Only their leaders exhibit moral failings; quarrels between nations are really only between governments, not peoples; secret diplomacy is immoral, though of course security secrets must be kept. Direct access to the people of other nations would solve all our diplomatic problems. For the people of these nations have basically moral goals—that is to say, our own. Yet leaders are as good as their followers make them, and every people has the government it deserves. This tissue of contradictory sentiments has nothing to do with the political realities of terror and indoctrination; of the helplessness of goodwill before a monopoly of violence; of the manipulation for political ends of prejudice, insecurity, and fear. Moralistic democracy never misses an opportunity to pay homage to the people; it is less concerned about opportunities to make the people worthy of it. We worship an idol fashioned in our own image, and risk the punishment of being condemned to live in a social order not of our own choosing.

The American morality of power is under continuous tension between our moralization and our vulgar pragmatism. The uneasy equilibrium between what we think of as "idealism" and "realism" periodically gives way to the one tendency or the other. Like a character in Dostoevski, we hang suspended between bursts of religious ecstasy and drunken debauchery. Power is to be used by men of conscience and integrity for the common good, and its exercise guided always by the ideals of justice and humanitarianism, sympathy and fair play. At the same time, power is intrinsically immoral, corrupting those who have it, and in its very nature destroying the freedom of those subjected to it. Politics, in short, we regard as a succession of necessary evils; we play with words to make virtues of these necessities, rather than apply our energies to reconstituting either the facts that make them necessary or the valuations that make them evil.

For the moralizer, power of any sort is a trust, public office an opportunity for public service. Nothing must be allowed to override the restraints on power of legality and conscience. Yet, Americans pride themselves on their toughness, too. Mercy is subordinated to justice, and justice in turn to public safety, especially under the rubric of national security. We must not coddle wrongdoers or be soft on our enemies. Though the ideal of power is service, politics is felt to be unsavory. Politicians, by and large, are incompetent; they are office hungry, and once they secure office will do anything to keep it; what they look for are sinecures or opportunities to exploit power for their personal advantage. From its beginnings American political thought has distrusted government, and this distrust has undeniably served to strengthen our freedoms. But while emphasizing the dangers of governmental interference we have also pictured government as foolish and ineffective, riddled with inefficiency, and incapable of coping with problems solved daily by private enterprise.

When power takes the form of actual violence, the American moral code condemns it unhesitatingly: violence is inadmissible as an instrument of policy. What can be identified as overt aggression is monstrous and shocking, regardless of provocations. (On the other hand, the drive for individual competitive success is admirable.) Our own military must be carefully watched to ensure its subordination to civil government; the military does not represent the nation, especially in peace time. Even in war, an all-out effort must still be subjected to moral restraints; total war belongs to totalitarianism. For all that, violence is justified and is even a duty when it is inflicted on an immoral enemy. In that case the war becomes a crusade; the Church Militant has the blessings of the Prince of Peace. Peace, after all, is secondary to righteousness. What is more, the fight against evil purifies its participants. During the past twenty years the acceptable American attitude toward Soviet institutions and practices has been a matter of delicate timing, not of realistic social analysis. A just war aims at nothing else than victory over the forces of evil; morality condemns any negotiated peace with aggressors—they must surrender unconditionally. Our military men, viewed "realistically," exhibit the acme of loyalty, courage, efficiency, and leadership. In short, violence is damnable, but the instruments of violence guarantee peace and are the symbols of security.

Symbols themselves may serve the ends of power. As such, they are thought to constitute "propaganda," which is vicious in its very nature: it deals in falsehoods, inflames political passions, and interferes with the right of the citizen to think for himself. Propaganda makes for conflict and confusion when it is used by the enemy; when used by us, however, it is largely without effect. On the other hand, it is necessary to refute the enemy's lies about us, and to compete with him for the friendship of neutrals. Besides, our own citizens must be indoctrinated with democratic ideals and principles. This is a matter of "education," however, not "propaganda." It must be scrupulously factual, limiting itself to providing the information from which the citizen can draw his own conclusions. The best propaganda is the simple truth; the facts can speak eloquently for themselves. Yet, not all the facts should be disseminated. A free flow of information is necessary so that the people can participate intelligently in the making of decisions; but military security, efficient governmental operations, and delicate diplomatic maneuvers all necessitate justifiable measures against excessive or ill-timed disclosures. A free press, of course, is a bulwark of democracy, provided it recognizes its public responsibility—that is, provided it is not divisive or so self-critical as to injure our standing in the eyes of other nations. In sum, the American code for political symbols, as for political practices and for the use of violence, allows us to keep our shining ideals untarnished in the parlor while we live our lives being "practical" in the kitchen.

In the conventional sense, the level of political morality in America is high. True, even conviction of a crime does not altogether preclude the holding of political office, including membership in the United States Congress.[63] And there are recurrent incidents in both major parties of bribery and corruption. But public morality in this sense only reflects the general level of morality in the country. Regardless of the quality of men in public service, no public officer, as Harold Ickes once pointed out, has ever bribed himself.[64] The point I have been urging, however, is that conventional political morality relates only to the externals of public policy, not to its substance. Policy honestly administered after having been formulated without undue influence by special interests is thought to raise no other moral issues. But it is just here that the important values are at stake, in the decisions made by honest men on behalf of what they sincerely believe to be the interests of those they represent.

The success we have so far attained in securing human rights and promoting social welfare—and it is considerable!—has too much inclined us to view our political and economic system as automatically guaranteeing moral achievement. Moral responsibility has too often been thought to be limited to keeping the mechanism in good working order; when it is running smoothly, moral values will take care of themselves. In the last few decades Americans have become widely aware of the moral bankruptcy in the totalitarian escape from freedom by submission to the will of the leader, the state, or the party. We are not yet equally conscious of our own moral escapism by submission to the will of the people as embodied in our political and economic institutions. We cannot restrain power by moral standards except as we free those standards themselves from amoral political restraints.

POLITICAL IDEALS

The substance of political morality relates to the content of public policy rather than to the honesty of its formation and administration. This substance is crystallized in political ideals—for America, as for the rest of the democratic world, in the classic ideals of liberty, equality, and fraternity. Whatever the failings in our conception of political morality, our practice with regard to these ideals justifies much of the praise we commonly bestow on it. I have little patience with the moralism that has eyes only for our shortcomings, never our achievements. Such moralism, especially in European appraisals, often invokes ideals only to rationalize a hostility to America whose motivation is far from ideal. Yet the misuse of criticism by others need not keep us from being critical ourselves. The point to which criticism must be directed is not, of course, the empty tautology that our actuality falls short of our ideals. It is, rather, that our moralistic misconception of these ideals continuously interferes with realistic moral achievement.

The most basic of the ideals is liberty, since it is not only an inherent value but is also instrumental to securing the others. To the Communists it is of no consequence, because in the perspectives of their historical determinism liberty is an illusion: individual choice is bound by historical necessity. To be sure, history does impose constraints on the individual; but it does not bind him altogether. Choice remains free within a range of possibilities that history provides. The past exerts a force that cannot be ignored, but it is not wholly irresistible. On the other hand, the metaphysical free will with which this determinism is frequently countered in America is equally irrelevant to action. Free choice is as subject to causality as is any other event. What makes it free is that among its causal agencies is included a symbolic indication of the future consequences of present alternatives. We are free when our choice is the product of full awareness of the needs to be met and of the resources and constraints of the situation in which we find ourselves.

Such psychological freedom is a necessary condition of political liberty. American dualism tends to view liberty as a matter either of political mechanisms or of "character" conceived in isolation from its formative elements in society. The emphasis we put on our tradition of freedom helps to overcome this dualism: tradition is constituted by both personality and institutions. It becomes a political force only as it constitutes in turn the basis of widespread participation in the political process. The importance of such participation for the maintenance of liberty has been recognized by political theorists since antiquity—most eloquently in Pericles' funeral oration. That the proportion of voters is lower in America than in most other countries does not necessarily signify a dangerous political apathy; it may also mark our contentment with the workings of our political system. Yet some measure of irresponsibility cannot be denied, or at least a sense of helplessness in the face of what is felt to be a vast and unmanageable political mechanism. "Go fight City Hall!" is as American as "You can't do this to me!"

In the last half century the development of depth psychology as well as the rise of authoritarian regimes has made Americans increasingly aware of the importance of personality in politics. The fact that thousands of ex-Nazis became Communists, as many ex-Communists turned to the authority of religion, we begin to find intelligible in terms of personality dynamics. The many studies of "the authoritarian personality" trace in character the roots of authoritarian institutions. Political liberty demands psychological independence, as against both conformism and rebelliousness; an integrated self, as against the internal conflicts of a dualistic code; and inner security, as against the neurotic quest for certainty that ends in absolutism. It is this dependence of political institutions on personality traits that justifies Dewey's insistence that democracy must be achieved anew by each generation.[65]

But freedom is a consequence as well as a condition of liberty. A purely psychological analysis is as inadequate as a purely institutional one. Independence is difficult to achieve in a society where the real dependencies of a complex division of labor are extended to the absurdities of reliance on "the expert" in every phase of life, and where "expertness" itself is only socially defined. Integration is not easy in a culture which unremittingly stimulates desire while withholding and even moralistically condemning what is necesary to its satisfaction. The insecurities that make this an age of anxiety owe as much to continuing economic and political uncertainty as to the traumas of personal history. This interdependence of free personality and libertarian institutions need not be seen as the working of a vicious circle of futility. It can equally be made the basis for a perspective of successive approximation.

The right of free speech may be viewed as uniting freedom and liberty in a single ideal. It is a right that is rooted in the core of personality by way of the beliefs and values for which it allows expression; and it reaches out to society in the act of expressing them through social channels. America still adheres, by and large, to the classic defense of this right, as formulated by Milton, Jefferson, Mill, and Holmes. The value of free speech is inherent as constitutive of the free personality, which cannot grow without expression. And it is of instrumental value in two ways, both as defending other liberties by allowing grievances to be heard and as necessary to the discovery of truth. Whatever truth authority may lay hold on is beyond correction if inquiry itself is subject to authoritarian control. And its truth cannot even be recognized outside of free inquiry, for there is nothing outside experience with which we can test its correspondence. The control of opinion, if it is not monstrously thorough, only dramatizes the forbidden belief. Like loyalty oaths, which are most oppressive on the most loyal, the denial of free speech, in creating a suffocating fear of heresy, robs even orthodoxy of its vitality. At this writing the public schools of our country's third largest city cannot freely discuss, for fear of undermining patriotism, an international organization which enjoys the active support of the Republic to which the patriot daily pledges allegiance.

Americans have been aware from the beginning of the dangers of political interference with their liberties, but we tend to overlook or underestimate the dangers outside the political mechanism. We recognize at once the viciousness in a pronouncement by the Communist Party on the correctness of a theory of genetics. We are not so quick in recognizing and resisting economic and social pressures on free opinion, whether from the monopolistic control of the mass media, the influence of advertisers, or the power of pressure groups. Not only the totalitarian governments have their captive audiences.

Yet it is, after all, the political factors that are basic to liberty, for the others are themselves subject to control by political power. Liberty in America derives from our constitutionalism. The legitimizing of power by the principle of representation leads to majority rule; it is the constitutional limits on power that guarantee minority rights. In detail, these limits constitute a system of juridical defense: innocence until guilt is proved; guilt for actions only, not for thoughts or intentions, and actions counter to predictable law, not to personal caprice; and the whole apparatus of due process of law. What this system comes to is the possibility of effective challenge to decisions. What makes challenge effective is our political pluralism—the existence of more than one party; the focusing of power in other institutions than the state; the press, the church, the unions, and organizations of every description; and the separation of powers within the state, for power can be limited only by power. In this respect the investigating committees of the past decade threatened our liberties in the act of trying to preserve them. They exercised all three powers of government at once: legislating by defining the offense of subversion, judging whether the offense had been committed, and punishing what they judged offensive by public defamation.[66]

The preservation of liberty thus requires the sharing of power by the citizenry. Conventionally, this is distinguished as the "positive" liberty which must supplement the "negative"; more accurately, it is a matter of a causal analysis supplementing a description of effects. The political mechanisms of universal suffrage, proportional representation, the initiative, referendum, and recall, and all the rest are only external marks of liberty. Its substance lies in access to the bases of control and the channels of influence in society: wealth, education, public office, media of communication, and the association of like-minded citizens into groups organized for common ends.

It is here that the fundamental problems of liberty in America must be localized. The individual alone cannot effectively counter the power to which he is subjected; he must organize with others. But the paradox of organization is that every organization acquires its own instinct of self-preservation, which drives it to sacrifice the principles for which it was established to the expediencies of its own survival. And the power within the organization, by what Michels called "the iron law of oligarchy," tends to become so concentrated as to threaten liberty anew. There is an even more pressing paradox within which democracy is caught up, the paradox of liberty: liberty itself must pay the price of more liberty. We must somewhere yield the right to choose in order to create a world in which elsewhere there is more right to choose. The continuing problem of democracy, for which no formula or mechanism can provide a permanent solution, is to find liberty *within* the system of power. Liberty must turn to power for resources as well as restraints. It is not enough to love liberty or any other political ideal; one must love with a maturity which is capable of living with the ideal as well as worshipping it.

The ideal of equality impressed de Tocqueville and countless other observers as most characteristically American. As a political ideal, equality of course is not a matter of personal attributes or possessions but of rights and opportunities. To be born equal is to be limited in opportunity only by native endowments and by restrictions universal in the society. The basic right of equality is to be taken into the community without conditions. The conception of separate but equal facilities is self-contradictory; the separatedness is itself an inequality. It is an exclusion from the community with an implied inferiority, a guilt by dissociation. Similarly, immigration quotas are defensible only when based on factors, like labor skills, relevant to a place in the community; formulated in terms of ethnic origins they betray the equalitarian ideal. There seems to be some confusion as to what is truly alien to the American spirit.

Equality of opportunity cannot be guaranteed once for all by any arrangement of the social mechanism. The stereotype of America as the land of unlimited opportunity did not derive from a literal absence of any limits; there have always been limits, and in the present century, old opportunities have vanished while new ones have come into being. What was felt to be important, what *is* important, is the equalization of whatever opportunities are available at any moment. This is not an automatic consequence of a pre-established harmony, as was postulated in classical economics; it calls for policy wisely directed to just that end. To be born equal is to be born with a right to contract freely for privileges by the free acceptance of duties, rather than into a determinate status of a fixed social order. But freedom of contract may become only a name if the pressure of economic necessity denies genuine choice. This is the significance of minimum-wage legislation and the apparatus of collective bargaining. As new pressures develop, new policies will be called for to maintain equality.

Equality is thus fundamentally an economic ideal as liberty is a political one and freedom a spiritual one. Of all the forms of discrimination, the economic has been judged to be the most serious, the most bitterly resented, and the one most markedly at variance with democratic ideals. Satisfaction of the primary economic needs is basic to an equalitarian society, for otherwise there is no genuine freedom to contract for further opportunities. These primary needs include more than food, clothing, and shelter; what the American economy can take pride in is its increasing recognition of the rights to educational betterment, productive work, and creative leisure.

Traditionally, the idea of equality has been conjoined with that of social justice, and they are still associated in the American moral code. We abhor the idea of "classes," so much so that it is difficult for us to consider it even as a category of purely descriptive social analysis; almost all Americans think of themselves as belonging to the middle class. To have no desire for getting ahead in the world, and especially for our children to be even better off than we are, is almost un-American. Social mobility in America is probably less than it was a century ago; but whatever the actuality, the aspiration remains. We are distrustful of the concentration of economic resources; moralistic support is always forthcoming for "the small businessman" and "the family farm." More effective is our determination to preserve equality with regard to values too important to be left to the inequities of economics—health, education, and the exercise of talent. Most Americans are prepared to meet the Communists on their own terms with the equalitarian ideal of a classless society.

An important component of this ideal is what Aristotle called "distributive justice," the distribution of goods on the basis of merit. To the American mind the bestowal of a privilege always evokes the question, "What has he done to deserve it?" Behind this colloquialism is Locke's justification of property by reference to the labor that was "mixed" with it in its production. Ownership is defensible only as it meets a moral obligation in terms of which it is judged to be deserved. The ideal of equality cannot countenance privilege which seeks justification only by allowing its benefits to trickle down to the less privileged. In a complex economy there is a correspondingly complex mixture of labor in all property. The continued attack by the extreme right on the income tax is met in the American moral consciousness with the insistence that the ability to pay is itself an index of benefits received: we pay the tax as the last obligation discharged in order to deserve the income.

What is at issue is the moral commitment of economic practice. But this commitment is only obscured in the moralistic dualism of "property rights" and "human rights." Property in the abstract is itself a human right; ownership is increasingly coming to be seen as a relationship among men, not between men and things. The entity that owns property is socially defined, even when we think it to be a concrete individual rather than an abstract corporation; and the fact of ownership consists of the enforcement by society of certain privileges of use. I say certain privileges, for the rights in property are in fact always far from absolute, however we verbalize them. The system of restrictions in force at any moment are taken to define the abstract and "natural" rights of property. When concrete values require changes in this system, such changes are either attacked as denying "property rights" or else defended in the name of contrasting "human rights." Morality does not call for a compromise between these spuriously contrasted claims, but for their integration in a humanized economy. Whether, how far, and in what respects our present economy should be subjected to planning, governmental controls, or even socialization, is a moral question, as are all questions of public policy. But it is not a moralistic one, which is to say, it is not a question of abstract principles. It is a question of concrete fact: how American values can best be achieved, in each situation as it arises, in accord with our own professed ideals.

The ideal of fraternity completes the classic trinity. "Democracy," Bryce wrote, "has not only taught the Americans . . . how to secure equality, it has also taught them fraternity. That word has gone out of fashion in the Old World. . . . Nevertheless there is in the United States a sort of kindness, a sense of human fellowship, a recognition of the duty of mutual help owed by man to man, stronger than anywhere in the Old World." [67] This is perhaps less true today than it was a century ago. A sense of human fellowship is a virtue of the frontier, and has almost vanished with the frontier. The conditions of urban life, even if they preserve the sense, provide few channels for its expression.

There is also a darker side to American history which must be faced. The history of bigotry in the United States is perhaps less shameful than in Europe, but not because it was any nobler in intent, rather, because it lacked the power to achieve its intent. Yet this in itself is a significant fact about American values. Bigotry today usually takes the form of prejudice by projection: "I myself am without prejudice, but unfortunately, my clients, employees, administrative superiors, . . . leave me no choice." A rationalization, to be sure; but by that very token a mark of acceptance of the ideal, even though it be an ambivalent acceptance.

There is no need to rehearse here once more the now familiar—alas, too familiar—explanation of prejudice in terms of scapegoating, insecurity, ego-enhancement, and the rest. More to the point is a recognition of the futility of the attempt to reinstate the ideal of fraternity on purely moralistic grounds. Too often the moralist bases his appeal for brotherhood on a reference either to a shared divinity or to the commonality of human nature: "After all, they're really just like us!" Such an appeal confuses community with identity, and reinforces prejudice by conceding the logic which derives a prejudicial conclusion from the premise of difference. To love another only because he is like me is to love not him but myself reflected in him; and to preserve my appearance I must at last destroy his reality.

Nor can fraternity be grounded in an appeal for "tolerance." This, too, concedes the implied objectionableness of difference and, what is worse, calls only for a passive permissiveness, not an active absorption of difference into the sense of community. There is an experiment in animal learning in which a hungry pike is put into a tank with minnows but separated from them by a sheet of glass. Again and again the pike dashes himself against the invisible glass, until he is conditioned to passivity. When at last the barrier is removed, the minnows can swim unmolested all around him. This is the state pictured by the philosophy of tolerance—live and let live. It cannot serve as an ideal for human society. In the relations of man to man, alienation and indifference may be even more disruptive of community than is hatred.

Perhaps the basic problem posed by the ideal of fraternity derives from the dehumanization of interpersonal relations in modern culture.

What is said in one of Silone's novels about fascist Italy comes uncomfortably near the mark with reference to the American business world: people do not have friends any more, only contacts and connections. Aristotle's *Ethics* devotes two long chapters to the goods of friendship; a comparably realistic treatise today would scarcely mention the subject. There may be widespread endorsement of Aristotle's dictum that "without friends no one would choose to live, even if he had all other goods." But its meaning is betrayed by our linking the goal of making friends to the goal of influencing people.

The depersonalization of politics is of particular relevance here. The bosses and ward heelers of the old-time machines related on a personal plane to the voters, and performed a variety of personal services for the large immigrant populations of the Eastern seaboard; the country candidate made himself personally known to his constituents. Today the mass media provide the channels for political appeal, and mere symbols of human relatedness replace the real thing—the nickname, the family pet, the image of the devoted wife. Such folksiness is of a piece with the moralistic verbalizations about brotherhood. In Plato's ideal *Republic* family life was to be replaced by a community structure in which every contemporary is a brother, every elder a father. Aristotle's criticism is refreshingly down-to-earth: "How much better is it to be the real cousin of somebody, than to be a son after Plato's fashion!" [68]

What part the state can play in sustaining the ideals of fraternity and equality is limited by its commitment to the ideal of liberty. But while prejudice may be politically inviolable, discrimination is not; at the very least, the state cannot be a party to discrimination by legally institutionalizing it. What more can be done America is now in the course of learning. The experimental temper of the American mind evokes both moralistic impatience and traditionalist denunciation. But in the long run nothing else than this temper can be relied on to ground our ideals in the realities of our daily life.

In American thought the ideals of liberty, equality, and fraternity are summed up in a single comprehensive ideal: individualism or, perhaps better, "individuality." Respect for the rights of the individual and recognition of his inherent worth imply all the rest. Democracy in America has conceived the values to be achieved by social action in terms of goods to be enjoyed in individual experience. Historically, this

but only as members of dubious organizations, and condemned not for their individual actions but for those of their guilty associates. We have undermined individualism in our anxious efforts to stamp out collectivist heresies, evoked insecurities in the name of security.

The paradox is that we have not taken individualism seriously enough. We are so preoccupied with preserving a way of life that we sometimes lose sight of the individuals living it. The words of de Tocqueville have a prophetic ring:

It would seem as if the rulers of our time sought only to use men in order to make things great; I wish that they would try a little more to make great men; that they would set less value on the work, and more upon the workman; that they would never forget that a nation cannot long remain strong when every man belonging to it is individually weak, and that no form or combination of social policy has yet been devised to make an energetic people out of a community of pusillanimous and enfeebled citizens.[69]

America's ideals of liberty, equality, and fraternity will yet make us strong—as individuals, not just as a nation, only if we have courage as individuals to face the realities of their pursuit.

METHODOLOGY OF MORALS

The formation of policy without regard to moral considerations is sometimes defended on the ground that the ethical principles on which public morality rests are a private matter and differ from person to person. There is no official ethics in America any more than there is an official religion. But agreement on ethics is not necessary for a moral consensus, just as differences in epistemology do not prevent acceptance of the same body of scientific truths. The same public morality can be grounded in a belief in God, man, or nature— at least sufficiently to make possible agreement on policy. Social philosophies are not expendable, but philosophers have each exaggerated the indispensability of their own social doctrine. Since Kant we have talked presumptuously of saving science or morality when it was our own philosophies that needed to be saved. Scientific and moral judgments are among the data of the philosophical problem; knowledge and valuation are the stuff of daily experience. A philosophy that ends by denying the existence of what it set out to explain reduces itself to absurdity. To be sure, the claim to knowledge and virtue in each particular case requires justification; and to formulate with philosophical adequacy what such justification consists in calls for the utmost care and subtlety. But we may know many things without knowing how we know them, and certainly without knowing much about the process of cognition itself. In America policy makers worry too much about philosophy, while philosophers do not worry enough about policy.

It is certainly true that not only its basis in ethical theory but also our moral knowledge itself is vague and unsure. But it is the part of an educated man, Aristotle says somewhere, to require exactness in each class of subjects only so far as the nature of the subject admits. If our requirements are realistic, we may even find that the situation is not so bad as in self-justification we are inclined to paint it. That the principles of public morality are far from definite and certain has not kept America, in a time of greatness, from applying them in public policy. The diagnosis in the *Federalist Papers* is still to the point:

Though it cannot be pretended that the principles of moral and political knowledge have, in general, the same degree of certainty with those of the mathematics, yet they have much better claims in this respect than, to judge from the conduct of men in particular situations, we should be disposed to allow them. The obscurity is much oftener in the passions and prejudices of the reasoner than in the subject. Men, upon too many occasions, do not give their own understandings fair play; but, yielding to some untoward bias, entangle themselves in words and confound themselves in subtleties.[70]

Morality is rarely a matter simply of applying an unquestioned principle to a case that indubitably falls under its scope. The moral problem is to weigh conflicting principles and to act on a balance of probabilities on behalf of the preponderant values. Totalitarian contempt for the democratic way of muddling through attacks precisely what is most defensible in our practice. Statesmanship is nothing other than muddling through; in politics the straight line is the shortest distance to perdition. To move unswervingly toward predetermined objectives is inevitably to bypass morality. Circumstances alter cases, and whatever be true of abstract principles, concrete moral values are nothing if not circumstantial. God Himself repented His creation when confronted by the generation of Noah. In a democracy, at any rate, policy must reconcile conflicting values, especially conflicting judgments of value, among the makers of policy. We talk too loosely of "government" and "the people" as though each were unitary and of a single mind. For government, the locus of moral issues is in such encounters as that of a secretary of state facing a senatorial hearing. For the people, it is in the encounters, not only among a multiplicity of overlapping groups but also within the individual, among the fragmentary selves whose integration is the achievement of moral maturity.

The desire for absolutes and the pretense of certitude are not a personal failing of American leaders. They are a constitutional weakness of democracy where everything turns on popular support. We do not often hear a politician admit that he has made a mistake. The politician, unlike the scientist, cannot rejoice in a disproved hypothesis, or he will do so in retirement from public life. But our predisposition to this weakness must put us all the more on our guard against it. To raise the level of public morality we must learn to tolerate a wider margin for error in public policy. If the spirit were not quite so willing the flesh might be not quite so weak.

I am not defending a particular political program that might be attacked as lacking in "idealism." I have no program to offer at all, and that is just my point: there is no such thing as a programmatic morality. When policy is wholly predetermined, moral values inevitably become absolute and abstract, and action is bifurcated into the amoralities of a vulgar pragmatism conjoined with an ineffectual moralism. In a democracy there are no recipes for the moral life. Democratic values can be defined procedurally, not by a content fixed beforehand. In terms of this procedure morality can be assimilated to science, in spite of the dualistic ethics which polarizes value and fact. Policy must be scientific to be effective; if morality is ineffective, it has no place in policy. But to say scientific is not to speak of the paraphernalia and techniques of the laboratory; it is to say realistic and rational—empirically grounded and self-corrective in application. Policy is scientific when it is formed by the free use of intelligence on the materials of experience.

American moralism has been so fearful of *realpolitik* that it has sometimes forgone being realistic altogether, especially in the field of foreign relations. Over and over again we have watched dictatorships rise, and even given them support, formulating our policies toward them by wishful thinking rather than by assessing consequences in the light of our past experience. We are realistic with respect to such limited and isolated objectives as obtaining military bases; but the larger values of peace and freedom we are inclined to pursue only by verbalizations. "If people loved humanity as genuinely as they loved their children," Bertrand Russell has recently said, "they would be as unwilling in politics as in the home to let themselves be deceived by comfortable fairy tales." [71] To be realistic does not mean resigning ourselves to the facts; it is not necessarily a matter of lowering our aspirations. The facts may also point to unrealized potentialities of value, to opportunities and resources as well as to limitations and constraints. The confusion of realism with resignation is a product of the childishness which complains that there is nothing to eat but food. When facts are prejudged as inimical to value, values are predestined to remain in the world of fantasy.

On a more fundamental level, moralists have argued that to ground values in the facts of experienced goodness is to reduce them to the crudities of desires as they are, not as they ought to be. It is to destroy morality by identifying it, at bottom, with nothing other than the satisfaction of animal instinct. In a democracy especially, realism, so the argument runs, subjects values to the vulgarization of the mass. This is the fallacious logic, however, which mistakes empirical science for a brute empiricism, as though respect for the facts precludes interpreting them, appraising their significance. A scientific hypothesis must stick to the facts, but it does so precisely by distinguishing them from superficial appearances. The realist bases judgments of value on what experience discloses to be good. But the disclosure requires assessment in the light of ideals that point beyond any given experience, though not beyond experience as a whole. The norms of the dictionary follow the facts of usage, but they are norms because there *is* such a thing as misusing words. Moral norms, if realistic, conform to the facts of experienced goodness; but there *is* such a thing as insensibility in the experience and irrationality in its assessment. When Aristotle says that political science does not make men but takes them from nature and uses them, he is a realist in what he affirms but not in what he denies. [72] Realistic politics must take men as they are at any given moment, but it must also create conditions in which men can grow to their full moral stature. In short, realism is not limited to the conservation of values already achieved; it can also aspire to the good which is not yet achieved. The realist will not leap into the void, but he is not for that reason earthbound.

Realism is above all contextualist. The distinctive quality of parlor politics, apart from its irresponsibility, is just this failure to refer issues to specific contexts. "Do you support a tough policy toward Russia?" is a meaningless question until both the toughness and the form of support are made concrete and specific. The lessons of operationism are as important for policy as for science: to be able to guide practice, theory must be formulated in terms that connect it with determinate behavior. The totalitarian criticism of the democratic state as a debating society is not altogether without substance. The floor of Congress has increasingly become a platform for empty verbalization; as the work of congressional committees becomes more responsive to its coverage by the mass media the same tendency appears. We face the serious problem of creating and maintaining conditions under which the issues of public policy can be realistically debated in public.

Contextualism implies not only that values can be appraised only in a concrete setting, but also that *there is always an appraisal to be made.* The moralist supposes that once the side of the right has been identified no further moral problems remain; there is left only the practical matter of ensuring that the right will prevail. What is good he supposes to be wholly good; there is no red ink in his ledger. If his dualism did not stand in the way, his moral judgment might benefit from a consideration of the practicalities of business enterprise. The operation of a business inevitably involves risks, and losses, too. Sound policy minimizes them but cannot eliminate them; simple prudence demands that they be carefully taken into account beforehand. This means a contextual appraisal, not a reliance on general and abstract principles. Weber's warning seems to me unanswerable:

No ethics in the world can dodge the fact that in numerous instances the attainment of "good" ends is bound to the fact that one must be willing to pay the price of using morally dubious means or at least dangerous ones— and facing the possibility or even the probability of evil ramifications. From no ethics in the world can it be concluded when and to what extent the ethically good purpose "justifies" the ethically dangerous means and ramifications.[73]

Morality desperately needs intelligence as well as virtue, good judgment as much as good intentions. It has seemed at times that our State Department was more concerned with sterling qualities of character than with ability. At the height of the Americanist purge an applicant for private employment was said to have admitted that he had been fired from the State Department, but he assured his prospective employer that it was only for incompetence! The Victorian advice, "Be good, sweet maid, and let who can be clever," is scarcely a foundation for twentieth-century morality. The sweet maids of today have found that they must be clever to remain good. In politics, at any rate, America cannot preserve its virtue unless it abandons its innocence. I am not making the Socratic identification of virtue with knowledge; but I do not see how we can hope to arrive at morally defensible policy unless we know what we are about. Our difficulties in foreign affairs surely stem in part from the fact that other nations are so often politically more knowledgeable than we are.

Granted that sometimes the morality of an action seems clear even when its consequences are not clear. This does not justify, however, the claim of moral intuition to be independent of such knowledge. What seems right may afterward turn out not to be so. Moreover, if our intuition is not mistaken, it is either our good fortune or else we are indebted to the cultivation of our intuition by what was already known to be right in the relevant circumstances. A scientific hypothesis may be assigned an antecedent probability prior to the outcome of the experiments by which it is tested. This is not an a priori probability, however, but one derived from the experience sustaining what has already been verified. What remains true is that often we know enough to recognize what is bad but, alas, not enough to recognize what is good. Here is where courage is called for—to be able to take thought without undermining the resolution to act. We need not choose between the yogi and the commissar or, in American terms, between the pedant and the goon. That an enterprise of great moment has been intelligently based on the best knowledge availible to us need not lose it the name of action.

When virtue is detached from knowledge it becomes easy for everyone to suppose that he already knows enough for the purposes of moral choice. It is in the American tradition for each man to be convinced that he has nothing to learn about politics, sex, or religion. But the conviction rings hollow, and in fact we are as a people unusually receptive to authoritative pronouncements on these matters by the experts. All three areas have their pundits, held in a popular esteem which can be given a rational justification only in very exceptional cases. Democracy does not presuppose that every citizen is an expert on morals nor does it necessarily succeed in making him one. But it does put the responsibility for moral choice on the individual citizen. The expert in a democracy must be only a consultant, not the decision maker. It is the citizen—directly and through his representatives—who must decide among conflicting expert opinions and how much weight to put on even a consensus of experts. Plato assigned this responsibility to a philosophical elite because only they, in his philosophical judgment, decided on the basis of thought, while the mass was swayed only by feeling. But the one duality is a reflected image of the other. The problem is as much to put feeling—responsible commitment to values—into the thought of the intellectual as it is to put thought—intelligent consideration of real conditions and consequences—into the feelings of the mass of the citizenry.[74]

It has become fashionable for the intellectuals to join with the less reflective members of the community in submitting to a religious or political absolute which can lighten the responsibility for individual moral choice. The position is still essentially Plato's: in his epistemology a proposition which is not universally and necessarily true is not knowledge at all but mere opinion. For Kant, universality and necessity are the criteria by which we can identify a priori principles, on which morality as well as science must rest. But the only such principles that have withstood the growth of knowledge and the changes in social patterns are those of pure mathematics. Logical analysis has shown, however, that pure mathematics pays for its absolute truth by sacrificing all its empirical reference. Judgments bearing on matters of fact can achieve no more than some degree of probability. What is hard to accept is that this probability suffices as a guide to life. Will men fight for a mere probability? They have and they will. A mature man does not demand ironclad guarantees from God or nature, and seldom even from other men; and surely he does not deceive himself with illusions of certitude to make bearable a life of uncertainty. Platitudinous though it be, there is profound wisdom in the Americanism that in this world nothing is certain but death and taxes. We do not always remember that Franklin wrote these words in a passage appraising the prospects of survival of the newly adopted Constitution. The courage of the men who established our republic was no whit lessened by their realistic perspectives on politics as a succession of calculated risks.

We often hear today the argument that "confused liberals" condemn absolute values as authoritarian and fascistic, while on the contrary the belief in such absolutes is necessary to the survival of democracy. The moralist urges again and again that our vulnerability to communism is basically "the collapse of our moral values," "the loss of faith in our principles," "the weakening of moral authority by the corrosion of scepticism." Heterodoxy in religious belief or in ethical theory is in some quarters condemned as downright subversive or dangerously near it. The ideals of democracy, it is insisted, are themselves absolute, distinguished from the absolutes of the authoritarian regimes in having been freely chosen rather than imposed by the state. According to this argument,

The crucial point is whether the absolutes are imposed from without or are voluntarily observed. Personal absolutes personally maintained are the essence of democracy and the antithesis of dictatorship. Freedom is itself one of the absolutes, a standard by which men can measure their lives, and only men who can maintain firm values can maintain freedom.[75]

Firmness in the maintenance of our values is one thing; the supposition that the values themselves must be unconditional and beyond question is quite another. The argument confounds the function of an absolute with its substance, its role in action with its status in nature. This confusion transformed Kant's empirical liberalism into Hegel's metaphysical authoritarianism. Ideas which Kant analyzed as regulative in experience the idealists treated as constitutive of a transcendent reality beyond experience. To say "standard" or "norm" is to say "functioning as an absolute"—used as a measure while not itself measured. But it functions as such only in that use, not intrinsically. As a result of its use, in other contexts it may itself be subjected to appraisal and modified or replaced. A standard is only a *relative absolute*, relative, that is, to the contexts of its normative function. Even the most basic principles of science are not eternal and unqualified truths, but instead the most powerful heuristic instruments so far known. A principle like that of the conservation of matter was for a long time presupposed in the design and interpretation of chemical experiments; but it itself rested on an experimental foundation, and indeed has been falsified in Einstein's identification of matter and energy. Cannot the "absoluteness" of the moral law be construed in the same way? I do not see how the values basic to a democratic social order are undermined when they are conceived as resting on an empirical basis. What is undermined is only the value theory which insists on construing these values as a priori, intuitive, and transcendental. It is not democratic morality that benefits from the absolutist's defense but only the absolutist's own ethics. To ground the value of freedom on all that experience has taught us of what is good for man in society is surely not to weaken its claims. And such a grounding points at once to the mode of connection of moral values with concrete political policy.

The absence of such a determinate connection is the most pressing objection to moral absolutism from the standpoint of its bearings on policy formation. I am directing attention to the futility of the belief that all moral problems have been essentially solved, and that the task for policy is only to translate these solutions into action. Where is the dictionary for such a translation? Just this is the problem; it is precisely in this task that statesmanship is called for. But here the moralist can make no contribution other than an exhortation to virtue. The American reputation for hardheadedness is well deserved by our rejection of panaceas for the social and economic core of public policy. But with regard to its moral penumbra, as we conceive it, we are, by contrast, extraordinarily simple-minded and naive. We tend to rely too much on the magic formulas of democratic theory. The maxim of the greatest good for the greatest number, for instance, is useless as a basis of choice when, as is almost always the case, one alternative provides a greater good for some while the other benefits more people though to a lesser extent; what, on this basis, is an equitable distribution of the tax burden? To take another example, reliance on the rule of the majority is not always even logically consistent, as has recently been demonstrated in a penetrating mathematical analysis of the theoretical relation between social choice and individual values.[76] And as a matter of practice the rule of the majority is certainly not always consistent with other democratic values. A few years ago an oriental under pressure to give up his home in a "restricted" residential area in a California city agreed to submit the question to a vote of the community; a majority voted against him. It is well said that there is no safety in numbers, or in anything else. In short, the moralist who can do no more than reaffirm his faith in the ideals of liberty, equality, and fraternity ignores the real problems occasioned by the use of one of these ideals to undermine the others.

Problems are also set by the necessity to compromise some of our values for the sake of the others, as in the paradox of liberty already mentioned. There is a comparable paradox of equality. The administrator of a public housing project may be concerned to break down a pattern of segregated housing in the community. But unless he himself imposes quotas on the occupancy of the public housing, the minority group which has been discriminated against, being under greater pressure, will fill the project completely, and instead of destroying segregation he will have contributed to it. But the quota is itself a discriminatory practice. Such dilemmas have no simple resolution, and certainly none in terms of abstract and absolute moral principles. In dilemmas of this kind, however, the moral problems of public policy largely consist.

There is no escaping the dependence of moral values on realistic contextual analyses of the situations in which they are to be secured or achieved. When Stephen Undershaft in Shaw's *Major Barbara* is interviewed by his father with regard to his career, he reveals neither aptitudes nor interests; but he does claim to know the difference between right and wrong. To which his father replies: "You don't say so! What! no capacity for business, no knowledge of law, no sympathy with art, no pretension to philosophy; only a simple knowledge of the secret that has puzzled all the philosophers, baffled all the lawyers, muddled all the men of business, and ruined most of the artists: the secret of right and wrong. Why, man, you're a genius, a master of masters, a god!" And when later in the scene Stephen identifies the power that governs England as "the best elements in the English national character," it is decided that he is a born journalist. In America he might have been recognized as destined to become a secretary of state.

American philosophy today must certainly share the blame for the sorry condition of contemporary thought about the relations of morals and policy. In the last few decades marked advances have been made in the empirical study and theoretical analysis of values, by such disciplines as anthropology, psychiatry, economics, and even mathematics. The contribution of philosophy to the understanding of social values has been slight. We have been preoccupied with the moral problems of the individual rather than with the problems of social ethics. Fifty years ago there was widespread agreement with Aristotle's dictum that "to discover the good of an individual is satisfactory, but to discover that of a state or nation is more noble and divine." [77] Today, except for occasional textbooks on "the conflict of ideologies," ethical treatises focus entirely on the analysis of a single paradigmatic moral judgment. Just as a political theory, however, cannot be appraised without regard to its moral consequences, so an ethical theory cannot be appraised without regard to its political implications. For the working morality which the ethical theory is intended to explain and justify is, under the conditions of modern life at least, inescapably political. As Croce has said, "Moral man does not put into practice his morality except by acting in a political manner and by accepting the logic of politics." [78] To have bearings on action ethics must take into account the social determinants of both the ends and the means of action. The fact that ours is preeminently the age of politics has not yet been sufficiently reflected in contemporary American philosophy.

What is worse, the philosophical theory of value seems to be completely caught up in the problem of subjectivism. There is a virtually exclusive preoccupation with the analysis of the justification for judgments of value. For two decades our philosophical journals have been filled with interminable discussions of whether value judgments are factual or only express the attitudes of the judger. The semantics and epistemology of ethics have been explored in detail, but not its specifically ethical content, and especially not the political bearings of such content. I do not mean that philosophers should abandon philosophy for politics; but I am pleading for a restoration of the social relevance of philosophy. We have focused so closely on the logical foundations that we are in danger of losing sight of the cultural superstructure which makes the foundations important.

It is true that philosophy has no special competence to deal with the problems of the superstructure. But it does have a special responsibility, surely as great as that of the journalist, priest, and psychiatrist to whom we have abandoned these problems. The philosophical task here, as I see it, is not to provide a "democratic ideology" or the "philosophical foundations" for such an ideology. It is to provide conceptual instruments which can be applied by the citizen himself to the materials of his own experience and the products of the human sciences so as to arrive at more realistic and intelligent perspectives on values in society.

CONCLUSION

The "moralist" whom I have been attacking is, of course, a fiction, as is every consistent representative of a philosophical position in all its purity. No life is limited to the concrete embodiment of a philosophical abstraction; the political behavior of living men and women is inevitably more subtle and complex than any political theory can pretend to picture. But the fiction is useful, nevertheless, as an "ideal type" in Max Weber's sense—a point of reference for the analysis of cases which all depart more or less widely from the type. If moralism has played too small a part in American policy for this reference point to be useful, so much the better! It is more useful than the usual fiction of the "materialist" who disregards moral values or pays them only lip service and who must therefore be enjoined to elevate his morality. That American policy leaves *something* to be desired from a moral point of view we can surely admit without compromising our loyalty. Democracy needs its critics today as much as its apologists. And for my part, what I find to criticize here is neither insensibility nor insincerity but rather their opposites. We have been so sincere in our devotion to the good that we have confronted the world in a posture of self-righteousness which we cannot maintain indefinitely without discomfort. There is no doubt, at any rate, that it makes other nations uncomfortable in their dealings with us.

As good a case can be made out for the charge against America of moralism as for the familiar charge of materialism. It is not that one myth will cancel out the other; both tendencies are at work and intensify rather than cancel one another. Walter Lippmann has recently held that

. . . the radical error of the modern democratic gospel is that it promises, not the good life of this world, but the perfect life of heaven. The root of the error is the confusion of the two realms—that of this world where the human condition is to be born, to live, to work, to struggle and to die, and that of the transcendent world in which men's souls can be regenerate and at peace. The confusion of these two realms is an ultimate disorder. It inhibits the good life in this world. It falsifies the life of the spirit.[79]

In essence, he is quite right. But perhaps the more radical error still is not in confusing the two realms but in conceiving them as two, in separating them at all. So long as they are distinguished, the good life on earth will inevitably be thought to derive from the perfect life of heaven, and the earthly city will either be abandoned to wickedness or else forced into the pattern of what is presumed to be the city of God.

It is in these dualistic perspectives that we supplement our moralism with a vulgar pragmatism. We promise earthly goods as well as heavenly ones, and often even deliver them. But having separated "practical" interests from "moral" ones, we find that even the fulfillment of the earthly promises fails to win us friends. Our philanthropies are suspected to conceal our self-interest, while the frank defense of our interests is condemned as immoral. In the minds of many people around the world, whatever the action, we are damned if we do and damned if we do not. In part, of course, it is Soviet diplomacy and propaganda that have maneuvered us into this position. But in part also, the extent to which they have succeeded points to the vulnerability of our own dualistic dilemma: what is moral is unreal, what is "realistic" is immoral. We may succeed, nevertheless, in establishing alliances, but we will not have friends among other nations. The transformation of an uneasy balance of power into a genuine international community must of course be a matter of slow growth, and our statesmen deserve the world's gratitude for every extension of time they can provide for this growth. But to make good use of our time we must extend and deepen our sympathetic understanding of other values, other ways of life.

What is genuinely pragmatic in America is our willingness to apply science to the problems of technology. Americans are widely stereotyped as having an intense and ever-present desire to improve ways of doing things, provided we see the improvement as only a change in means for established ends. But it is true that with regard to ends we are remarkably conservative. The scientific outlook of our technology continues to undermine traditional conceptions of value, but that outlook is usually regarded as incapable of replacing those conceptions by more adequate ones. The achievement of nuclear fission has not suddenly made science a threat to civilization. It has only stepped up the magnitude and urgency of a problem faced by civilization since science first became a significant force in society. Some years before the atom bomb Dewey wrote: "A culture which permits science to destroy traditional values but which distrusts its power to create new ones is a culture which is destroying itself." [80] Not science itself but the leaden shield that insulates it from ethics and politics is deadly. We must either leave science alone altogether and forgo its transformation of means, or else integrate it with our moral aspirations and forgo the fixity of traditional ends. This is the spirit in which I have been urging a realistic political morality, which is to say, a continued reassessment of traditional moral values in the light of contemporary political actualities. A belief is not scientific because it has been "proved" but because it is continuously tested, and tested by conformity to experience rather than to axiomatic truths. It is in this spirit, too, that I have pressed the claims of an empirical, naturalistic theory of value. An ethics which provides a religious or metaphysical foundation for political morality has still to solve the problem of bringing that morality into connection with the world of political action revealed in experience.

I have viewed political morality, therefore, as a matter of proximate choices, not of ultimate goals. It is customary to criticize politicians for lacking statesmanlike vision; statesmanship, however, consists in seeing clearly what here and now bears on long-run values. Communism has plenty of vision—focused on a utopian future, but not on the miseries and brutalities of the present. American moralists may be equally visionary when they prefer the ultimate virtue of uncompromising principle to the day-to-day gains of a compromised good. "The path of duty lies in what is near, and men seek for it in what is remote." What a political realist Confucius was! Political morality lies in the everyday shaping of policy, not merely in the heroic stand at a time of crisis. The association of morality with heroism and martyrdom is not intrinsic to morals, but is a part of the contemporary crisis mentality. We talk so much of "the crisis of our time" that we come to think that some single stroke of statesmanship will put an end to our problems—one way or the other— once for all. I do not believe that the atom will destroy all life on earth, nor do I believe that the latest Peace Plan will forever remove its destructive potentialities. I do not believe in the Apocalyptic Moment in politics: every day is the Day of Judgment. In the politics of crisis law and morality are both endangered.

I have attacked conformism, not because I reject the values pressed upon us but because the pressures interfere with the realistic appraisal of values. Even when the conformist judgments of value are sound, they can scarcely lay claim to rationality; for rationality cannot be defined by the content of belief but only by the procedure for arriving at the content. What is worse, conformism has an appetite for power that grows by what it feeds on; orthodoxy has devoted itself more and more only to the stamping out of heresy. Political morality depends on voices of protest. To silence them is not only an immorality in itself but also makes for other immoralities as policy becomes exempt from critical appraisal. We rightly condemn Communist "elections" in which there is only one set of candidates; but many Americans take for granted that only one set of values suffices for democratic choice.

Quite apart from the possibility of public protest, we must surely allow for private reservations. The individual must be able to find a refuge from the conformist pressures of society. "The right to be let alone," Brandeis has said, "is the most comprehensive of rights and the right most valued by civilized men." In American life this right is continuously threatened, not so much by political instrumentalities as by the more subtle invasions of privacy in a variety of social patterns and practices. The teacher, the business executive, the government employee, and even the research scientist are all subjected to a code of conformity whose requirements increasingly extend beyond the range of their professional activities. Competitive advertising has been attacked many times for its wastefulness and its degradation of public taste. More fundamental is its weakening of our sense of the right to be let alone, to live our lives as we choose. It is not what the advertiser says, but the frequency and intensity with which he says it, the inescapability of his urging, which is truly degrading.

When the conformist directs himself to the preservation of "Americanism" his efforts are self-defeating. More and more his "American" comes to be defined only negatively, as a noncommunist. Our prestige abroad may suffer more from this negativism than from the stupidities and injustices with which the negative definition is applied. It offers nothing to the neutrals save the assurance that if they join us they will be on our side. But *what* side is it? It is not surprising that other nations think of us as materialists: it is our materials that we most freely export. As for our values, when we have descended from the clouds of moralistic generalities, they are not clear in our own minds; in that condition, we can hardly expect to be able to state them clearly to others. And, above all, our values are not clearly embodied in our actions. De Maupassant tells a story of a young man challenged for the first time to a duel, who is thrown into such an agony of fear of the outcome that on the morning of the duel he takes his own life. Negative "Americanism," by a kind of defensive subversion, destroys what it is most fearful of losing. I do not mean to say that if we conquer our fears our problems will vanish. The problems of democracy are rooted in more than our own anxieties; we now have more to fear than fear itself.

The preservation of liberty calls for leadership, as important in democracy as in the totalitarian states. Edmund Burke long ago called attention to the paradox of representation: the representative owes his constituency his own judgment as well as a representation of their will. The demands of democratic leadership cannot be side-stepped by policies aimed at giving the people "what the people want." America has had world leadership thrust upon it, it is often said, and the next century may look to the Pax Americana as the last one looked to the Pax Britannica. The problem is to outgrow our political adolescence in time to discharge this mature responsibility.

The ideal of equality confronts us with the continuing task of operating our economy in the general welfare, which means recognizing all the special interests that make up the generality, without identifying the general welfare with any one of them—even the special interest of General Motors. We cannot side-step this problem by a verbalistic appeal to an abstract "national interest" unrelated to the needs of concrete individuals. "The art which discovers the public interest by eliminating the interests of successive sections of the public," Tawney once pointed out, "smacks of the rhetorician rather than of the statesman." [81]

The problems of fraternity, finally, are not solved by desegregation alone; it is integration that is called for, the creation of genuine community, both nationally and internationally.

What gives all these problems a peculiarly moral cast is that they are constituted by man's relations to man. We need not share Schopenhauer's pessimism to recognize that "the chief source of the evils which affect men is man himself." The real world, he continues, "surpasses Dante's hell in this respect, that one man must be the devil of another." [82] Moral revivalism will not suddenly transport us from hell to heaven. When we have solved one moral problem, another will arise to take its place; the Divine Comedy plays forever in the second act.

All this will probably be regarded by many as nothing but old-fashioned liberalism which has long ago been exploded. But the the old-fashioned liberalism was victimized by the dualism of ideal aspirations and material interests, it was given to moralization, and it tended to absolutism with regard to its own values. Laski's characterization seems to me a fair one:

> Liberals viewed Americanism less as a concept of power than as a concept of ethics. They still thought . . . that there was a natural law, expressive of a natural order, which man breaks at his peril. . . . They still laid . . . far more emphasis on the free individual than upon the free society. They retained the illusion of a security for the American which could be enjoyed by all other peoples if they would only exercise the virtues of reason and goodwill. And there was an inner conviction, inevitably strengthened by their sense of overwhelming power, that it was their mission to lead the world to righteousness. They still had, despite the experience of two world wars, what Emerson called "the disposition to trust a principle more than a material force." [83]

But I have been as critical of *this* liberalism as of the political philosophies it set itself against. My aim has been to reinstate the connection between morality and power, to give political force to moral principle.

If, nevertheless, it is felt that the position of this essay is old-fashioned liberalism still, I will not protest too much. If it is a matter of labels, I do not mind being politically identified as a pre-Raphaelite. We are all of us living on the moral capital of the liberalism of a generation or two ago, whether or not we find it politically expedient to acknowledge the source of our riches. Whatever its shortcomings, it is the old-fashioned American dream that brought America moral greatness. There was a time when we said to the nations of the world, "Give me your tired, your poor, your huddled masses yearning to breathe free." Today this is embarrassing sentimentality. And it is even more embarrassing politically, for it is written on the Statue of Liberty but nowhere to be found in our immigration code. Simple decency—to say nothing of the friendship of other peoples—demands that we remove it from the one or restore it to the other.

I am myself an immigrant, from a family of immigrants, and I see America still as those huddled masses saw it—so various, so beautiful, so new. When my father visited Washington for the first time, I stood with him under the dome of the Capitol and watched what he saw of America struggling with what he remembered of tsarist Russia. Then he asked, "Does it really belong to us?" It does indeed—it belongs to the people, to all the people—if we but choose to make it our own.

NOTES

[1] Cotton Mather, *Diary*, 1716; quoted by Harold J. Laski, *The American Democracy* (New York: Viking, 1948), p. 432.

[2] Max Weber, *The Protestant Ethic and the Spirit of Capitalism* (Chicago, Ill.: University of Chicago Press, 1930), p. 87.

[3] George Santayana, *Character and Opinion in the United States* (New York: Doubleday, 1956), p. 103.

[4] This appears to be belied by R. W. Davenport and the editors of *Fortune:* "The American character and tradition will never be satisfied with a merely defensive or even preventive foreign policy. We seek ways to be creative and constructive. . . ." *U.S.A.: The Permanent Revolution* (New York: Prentice-Hall, 1951), pp. 249–250. But the passage continues: ". . . ways in which we can feel we are extending the American Proposition [*sic!*] to other peoples." It is not this extension that I had in mind by an "ideological offensive."

[5] Walter Lippmann, *The Public Philosophy* (New York: Mentor, 1956), pp. 80, 123, and throughout; Benedetto Croce, *Politics and Morals* (New York: Philosophical Library, 1945), p. 145; John Dewey, *German Philosophy and Politics* (New York: Holt, 1915), p. 44; Jacques Maritain, *Man and the State* (Chicago, Ill.: University of Chicago Press, 1951); Zevedi Barbu, *Democracy and Dictatorship* (New York: Grove, 1956), p. 58.

[6] Charles Stevenson, *Ethics and Language* (New Haven: Yale University Press, 1947).

[7] UNESCO, *Human Rights: Comments and Interpretations* (London: Allan Wingate, 1949), p. 11.

[8] Charles E. Merriam, *Political Power* (New York: McGraw-Hill, 1934), p. 113.

[9] James Bryce, *The American Commonwealth* (New York: Macmillan), vol. 2, p. 278; Gunnar Myrdal, *An American Dilemma* (New York: Harper, 1944).

[10] See George R. Stewart, *American Ways of Life* (New York: Doubleday, 1953), pp. 69–70.

[11] Bryce, op. cit., p. 632.

[12] *Job*, XXXI, 13–15.

[13] "The number of human beings sacrificed in late prehistoric and historic times must be reckoned in thousands of millions, all of them immolated to the gods in behalf of the welfare of the community." Homer W. Smith, *Man and His Gods* (New York: Grosset and Dunlap, 1956), p. 134.

[14] See, for instance, M. J. Hillenbrand, *Power and Morals* (New York: Columbia University Press), 1949, p. 69: "No system of political ethics which demands the obedience of men on the basis of moral obligation can have validity unless it involves

108

certain concepts which, taken together, equal the natural law, no matter how reluctant men are to use that designation."

[15] Jeremy Bentham, *Introduction to the Principles of Morals and Legislation* (New York: Oxford, 1923), p. 18 n.

[16] John Dewey, *Freedom and Culture* (New York: Putnam, 1939), p. 29.

[17] John Dewey, "Theory of Valuation," *International Encyclopedia of Unified Science*, vol. 2, no. 4 (Chicago, Ill.: University of Chicago Press, 1939).

[18] C. I. Lewis, *An Analysis of Knowledge and Valuation* (La Salle, Ill.: Open Court), 1946.

[19] Dewey, *Freedom and Culture, op. cit.*, p. 104.

[20] J. Ortega y Gasset, *The Revolt of the Masses* (New York: Mentor, 1950).

[21] W. E. Lecky, *History of European Morals* (New York: Appleton, 1929), vol. 1, p. 88.

[22] Jacques Barzun, *God's Country and Mine* (Boston: Little Brown, 1954), p. 90.

[23] Bryce, *op. cit.*, vol. 2, p. 458.

[24] Santayana, *op. cit.*, p. 27.

[25] Quoted by David Riesman et al., *The Lonely Crowd* (New York: Doubleday, 1953), p. 200.

[26] Quoted by D. W. Brogan, *The American Character* (New York: Vintage, 1956), pp. 75–76.

[27] Laski, *op. cit.*, p. 738.

[28] Davenport, *op. cit.*, p. 19.

[29] Riesman, *op. cit.*, pp. 207–208.

[30] Barzun, *op. cit.*, p. 81.

[31] Job, I, 9–10.

[32] Alexis de Tocqueville, *Democracy in America* (New York: Longmans, 1889), vol. 2, p. 179; see also Brogan, *op. cit.*, p. 16.

[33] Martin Lipset, "The Sources of the 'Radical Right,'" in Daniel Bell (ed.), *The New American Right* (New York: Criterion, 1955), p. 224 n.

[34] Max Weber, "Politics as a Vocation," in H. H. Gerth and C. Wright Mills (eds.), *From Max Weber* (New York: Oxford, 1946), p. 120.

[35] Laski, *op. cit.*, p. 737.

[36] Barzun, *op. cit.*, p. 113.

[37] Aristotle, *Nicomachaean Ethics*, I, 1097 a.

[38] Compare also Aristotle's dictum: "The time when, and the cases in which, and the persons towards whom, and the motive for which, and the manner in which, constitute the mean and the excellence."

[39] Bryce, *op. cit.*, vol. 2, p. 477.

[40] Oliver Wendell Holmes, "Natural Law," in his *Collected Legal Papers* (New York: Harcourt Brace, 1921). The passage continues: "It seems to me that this demand is at the bottom of the philosopher's effort to prove that truth is absolute and of the jurist's search for criteria of universal validity which he collects under the head of natural law. . . ."

[41] Santayana, *op. cit.*, p. 106.

[42] Quoted by Carl L. Becker, *Freedom and Responsibility in the American Way of Life* (New York: Vintage, 1955), p. 51.

[43] Dewey, *Freedom and Culture, op. cit.*, pp. 90–91. He continues: "Arbitrary irresponsibility varies in direct ratio to the claim for absoluteness on the part of the principle in behalf of which power is exercised."

[44] Compare Daniel Bell, *op. cit.*, p. 17: "Throughout our history, Americans have had an extraordinary talent for compromise in politics and extremism in morality. The most shameless political deals (and 'steals') have been rationalized as expedient and realistically necessary; yet in no other country were there such spectacular at-

tempts to curb human appetites and brand them as illicit—and nowhere else such glaring failures."

[45] Laski, *op. cit.*, pp. 719–720.

[46] H. D. Lasswell, *Psychopathology and Politics* (Chicago, Ill.: University of Chicago Press, 1930); *World Politics and Personal Insecurity* (New York: McGraw-Hill, 1935).

[47] See James Burnham (ed.), *What Europe Thinks of America* (New York: John Day, 1953), p. 43.

[48] Bryce, *op. cit.*, vol. 2, p. 278.

[49] William James, *The Principles of Psychology* (New York: Holt, 1927), vol. 2, p. 549.

[50] Weber, "Politics as a Vocation," *op. cit.*, p. 118.

[51] A. Valentine, *The Age of Conformity* (Chicago, Ill.: Regnery, 1954), p. 177.

[52] Compare Daniel Bell, *op. cit.*, p. 20: "The singular fact about the Communist problem is that an ideological issue was raised in American political life, with a compulsive moral fervor only possible because of the equation of Communism with sin. A peculiar change, in fact, seems to be coming over American life. While we are becoming more relaxed in the area of traditional morals . . . we are becoming moralistic and extreme in politics."

[53] Bryce, *op. cit.*, vol. 2, p. 273.

[54] Santayana, *op. cit.*, p. 106.

[55] James Madison, *Federalist Papers*, No. XIV.

[56] Nathan Glazer and Martin Lipset, "The Polls on Communism and Conformity," in Bell, *op. cit.*, p. 145.

[57] Santayana, *op. cit.*, p. 104.

[58] Barzun, *op. cit.*, p. 99.

[59] Quoted by Laski, *op. cit.*, p. 747.

[60] Bryce, *op. cit.*, vol. 2, p. 352.

[61] See, for instance, Sidney Hook, *Toward the Understanding of Karl Marx* (New York: John Day, 1933).

[62] Compare Croce, *op. cit.*, p. 188: "Whenever we hear someone refer to 'historical necessity' rather than to his conscience to justify an impending decision about some line of action, we can be sure that we are faced with a case of lack of moral sensibility, or with an attempt to defraud the uncheatable law of duty."

[63] See George A. Graham, *Morality in American Politics* (New York: Random House, 1952), p. 89 and throughout.

[64] Quoted by Graham, *ibid.*, p. 49.

[65] John Dewey, *Problems of Men* (New York: Philosophical Library, 1946), p. 39.

[66] See Alan Barth, *The Loyalty of Free Men* (New York: Pocket Books, 1952).

[67] Bryce, *op. cit.*

[68] Aristotle, *Politics*, II, 3.

[69] De Tocqueville, *op. cit.*, vol. 2, p. 301.

[70] Alexander Hamilton, *Federalist Papers*, No. XXXI.

[71] Bertrand Russell, *The Impact of Science on Society* (New York: Simon and Schuster, 1953), p. 87.

[72] Aristotle, *Politics*, I, 10.

[73] Weber, "Politics as a Vocation," *op. cit.*, p. 121.

[74] Compare Dewey: "The conclusion is not that the emotional, passionate phase of action can be or should be eliminated in behalf of a bloodless reason. More 'passions,' not fewer, is the answer. To check the influence of hate there must be sympathy, while to rationalize sympathy there are needed emotions of curiosity, caution, respect for the freedom of others."

[75] Valentine, *op. cit.*, p. 174.

110

[76] Kenneth Arrow, *Social Choice and Individual Values* (New York: Wiley, 1951).

[77] Aristotle, *Nicomachaean Ethics*, I, 2.

[78] Croce, *op. cit.*, p. 24.

[79] Lippmann, *op. cit.*, pp. 109–110.

[80] Dewey, *Freedom and Culture*, *op. cit.*, p. 154.

[81] R. H. Tawney, *The Acquisitive Society* (New York: Harcourt Brace, 1920), p. 135.

[82] Schopenhauer, *The World as Will and Idea* (London: K. Paul, 1896), vol. 3, p. 388.

[83] Laski, *op. cit.*, pp. 736–737.